Achevé d'imprimer le 24 septembre 1994
sur les presses de
Publi off 7
Maquette et composition
PEMA. HENRI BERGER PRODUCTIONS — Paris
Dépôt légal 4e trimestre 1994
Photo de couverture : J. B. — Paris

Ce livre a été tiré à 50.000 exemplaires
dont 100 exemplaires numérotés (hors commerces)
et 10.000 exemplaires en anglais.

H.COM.I.E. et V.A.C.

Translated from the French by
Kristi Essick and Gonzalo Moreno
December 1994

•

Romania at the Moment of Truth

ION ILIESCU

Romania at the Moment of Truth

ÉDITIONS
HENRI BERGER

Foreword

The following pages are not "memoirs," even if, in certain places, they seem to be. They do not claim to broach all of the problems posed by the Romanian Revolution which is a very controversial and complex phenomenon. Nor do they answer all of the often dramatic questions brought about by an event of such magnitude. Nonetheless, it is timely for me to express my feelings concerning the meaning of this Revolution, convinced that the path taken is now irreversible, and to express my point of view on the reforms in progress and on the transition period we are currently in. Revolution and reform, it seems to me, are the most significant terms used to evoke the evolution of a country put to brutal tests by History since the beginning of its existence.

More a political meditation and the story of a personal journey than a description of precise situations and facts, this work aims to aid understanding of our Revolution through my own vision of the events into which I was thrown through extraordinary circumstances.

Two principles guided the creation of this book:
1 - To highlight the particular events of the Romanian Revolution in the context of the changes that continue to shake Central and Eastern Europe;
2 - To attempt to evaluate Romania's development in terms of the political, social and economic transformations in the world today.

One last comment: my dearest wish is to be able to remain that which I have always been, a man who lives among and side by side other men, always ready to listen and to try to understand. Certainly, power insidiously changes those who exert it and the only constraint to this is a continual and ever-changing relationship with the people. I am not afraid of the booby-traps of power; the cold and formal protocol which surrounds me bothers me and I avoid it at all costs. Writing this book was a true "escape," a different way to reach the reader whom I invite to look at Romania from a new perspective, to come to know it a little better and to consider the painful journey that it has had to endure in order to gain freedom and a democracy worthy of the norms and values of contemporary society. I hope to give the reader the impression that my country has every reason to believe in its future.

I have absolute faith in my country's capacity for regeneration. Romania is changing for the better.

The December 1989 Revolution and the Birth of a New Power

The Revolution: an Explosion

At 12:06 PM on December 22, 1989, Nicolae Ceaucescu boarded a helicopter on the roof of the Romanian Communist Party Central Committee. He had ruled Romania for the last 25 years, and was now fleeing under the threat of a raging crowd which was storming his headquarters down below.

The Romanian Revolution had triumphed. Our joy was overwhelming.

How did we get there? Why was Romania only able to get rid of its Communist regime through force and violence? How is the Romanian Revolution related to the other changes which occured in this part of the world? What are its own characteristics? How is it different from the changes that have disrupted Eastern and Central European societies? How do these changes resemble the Romanian Revolution?

In fact, the Romanian Revolution was a social eruption with a strong national and popular flavor. It quickly reached an explosive stage, in a few days in Timisoara, in a few hours in Bucharest, from where the fire rapidly spread to set ablaze nearly all of the country's most significant cities. We couldn't treat ourselves to the luxury of a "Velvet Revolution," primarily because of an unbending Communist regime which, in its last few years, had blocked all initiatives (indeed intentions) aimed at political and social reform. Only a dramatic revolution could change such a frozen situation. The joy of having succeeded was tarnished by our mourning for those who had sacrificed their lives to make this victory possible.

The forms of resistance to the Ceaucescu dictatorship were numerous, ranging from the silent hostility of the people to the open protests by a certain number of notable, isolated intellectuals who never managed to organize themselves. Their acts of courage remained confined in small elite circles, without ever reaching a wider audience nor persons who could have pressured the government to implement political reform. In this situation, the Romanian Revolution lacked the vital fuel that prepares such an event and assures not only its success but especially its future: a detailed program with clearly defined goals, the organization of the different social forces taken to victory and called upon to join in these goals, and sufficiently charismatic leaders to focus the will of the people and to steer collective actions. Just when everything was toppling in our neighboring countries, Romania remained an isolated island, completely excluded from the possibility of change.

Looking back today at the Romanian Revolution enables us to better understand its paradoxical unfolding. True, no one had foreseen such a rapid and radical collapse of the Communist regimes; even the most informed analysts had been caught by surprise. Yet it was clear that totalitarian regimes no longer had a future in this part of the world. But Nicolae Ceaucescu did not seem to understand, and his blindness, or his stubbornness, made our victory more costly.

The characteristics of our revolution stem from the specific conditions of a country where the power structure had succeeded in dissipating and neutralizing not only the forces which could have made up a political opposition within the country, but also civilian society, where the seeds for an alternative could appear and grow. True, geopolitical factors played a role, but in contrast to what happened in neighboring countries, the Romanian Revolution took place in a vacuum, without any preliminary build-up. It wasn't the culmination of a series of events leading to radical change, but rather the critical point for a society frozen by an oppression whose only outlet for the increasingly violent social tensions was to be an outright explosion.

Conspiracy and Manipulation?

After all that has been said and written about the December 1989 Romanian Revolution, the accounts of even the most reliable witnesses, who can offer original facts and spectacular revelations, stand a good chance of being disappointing. The most surprising aspect for events of such a scope is exactly the simplicity and the manner in which the new power was born in the confusion, through the twists and turns of History. It is difficult to imagine that change as profound as that which led Romania from dictatorship to democracy could not have been the result of a conspiracy, of hidden scheming, of a pre-established scenario, or of any kind of manipulation.

A government overthrown from within, capable of sparing the country the convulsions of a revolution, would have meant the gratitude of History and the status of heroes to those who would have led it. I was not the only one to consider it, but did not succeed in implementing a political structure capable of bringing about the changes that the entire country was desperate for. At no time did I consider calling for help from a foreign power, nor did I resort to scheming which I cannot openly talk about today. All talk concerning this is gratuitous, clearly showing bad faith, unless, of course, it's the burning imaginations of a few sensationalistic journalists.

I have always refuted the baseless claims which alleged that the Romanian Revolution was only a conspiracy. To look at things in such a way excessively simplifies the logic and the development of events, in which the principal protagonist was the crowd of protesters that poured out onto the streets to express the desperation of a people determined to do away with the dictatorship. A phenomenon of such a magnitude cannot be explained away in scenarios concocted by various foreign intelligence services, and used by people whose only aim was to seize power. Such scenarios may very well have existed. In view of the relentlessness and the persistence with which certain political circles inside and outside the country are trying today to again rehash the idea of a "confiscated" revolution, or of a "coup d'état", and considering the efforts made since the Revolution to keep me away from power – even to prevent me from running for office in 1990 and 1992 – I am tempted to give some credit to a comment someone once made to me: "Sir, your appearance on the political scene certainly foiled the plans of those who had different ideas for Romania. That explains the hatred that they have for you, and will continue to have for you as long as you have power." Yet what prevented a scenario like this from happening was not my presence or anyone else's, but rather the size of the popular movement which made any manipulation impossible. The massive spontaneous uprisings resemble a ground swell which, through its whirlwinds, brings about diverse, often surprising, destinies. This was my case.

In the first four years after the Revolution, I was exposed to many attacks and attempts to discredit me, coming from the right-wing as well as from the left-wing media, everyone rallying around the same political program and whose only watchword was "Down with Iliescu." I also noted repeated and diligent efforts to divert the Revolution's direction, to retrace its development and history, starting with biased and impartial points of view. A large number of those on the political scene also used the Revolution as an umbrella to protect their various interests, attempting to shape its image around the defense of these interests and did so without respect for those who had sacrificed their lives.

My own thirty years of public service – over time, the previously committed communist that I was turned into its political opponent – gave me a certain notoriety allowing me to represent hope for both those who envisioned the change of the regime and for those who were frightened by this perspective. I wanted to use this to my advantage to establish a relationship among those like me who were inclined to believe that it was necessary to act in order to limit the dictatorship's excesses and to clear the way for reforms within the system. But I had to admit very quickly that the condition Romania was in did not allow for a "Velvet Revolution" and the capital of confidence into which I was investing would only prove to be useful at the moment when the popular uprising needed it to transform a social explosion into a political gain.

Likewise, foreign pressure certainly attempted to destabilize Ceaucescu's dictatorship without ever really being able to shake it.

I knew that once launched, a revolution could neither be stopped nor diverted; it follows its course against all opposition. At the time, I was unaware of the media's fundamental importance, which plays a decisive role in the perception of events, especially concerning facts as exceptional as those which we were experiencing.

Reality was continually distorted by a media version. What people perceived inside and outside the country, everywhere in the world, was not facts, but an often roundabout image that the media put forth. This image was manipulated and distorted by over-simplification and an appetite for the sensational, unrelated to what I knew to be truthful or even plausible. Even today, there remains a gap between Romanian reality and the image portrayed by certain members of the media. It was the "the first televised revolution." This generated on one hand an immense amount of sympathy and a generous outpouring of support, and on the other hand, such enormous distortions that I often wondered if they were not just outright lies.

Manipulation – notably media-related, with the most far-fetched information having been circulated at the start of the Revolution – certainly had an emotional impact and probably hastened some of our actions in unnecessary ways. Each individual was under the emotional spell aroused by the 60,000 alleged victims announced by foreign press agencies, a number very different from reality (the real number of deaths being already dramatic enough) but which we accepted at face value. Everyone felt threatened by the helicopter formations and the machines of war that apparently only existed in certain people's imaginations (even if army radars actually registered some abnormal signals). Diversions of this kind played no role, neither in the launch of the popular movement, nor in the decisions made by those whom the movement placed in power. In short, to understand the revolution – and also the Romania born of this social and political upheaval – nothing is as important as an account chronicling the facts in all of their stunning simplicity: a sudden eruption of favorable circumstances which were, however, not lacking ambiguities. This political work steered Romania in a direction which was not the clearest at the time, but which was certainly right, because since then, several elections and the development of Romanian society have proved this to be so.

The Unravelling of Power

The events in Timisoara, which set off the Romanian Revolution, provoked an immense reaction throughout the country, which had long awaited a clearly inevitable explosion.

The power structure itself was caught off-guard, though I find it hard to believe that it had not noticed the writing on the wall and not understood the people's worries and torments. It committed the error of taking the people's resignation for fear; and worse, for a sign of affection and approval. Moreover, those at the summit of power protected themselves with impenetrable layers from the economic disaster for which they were responsible. Disgraceful in its stature, Nicolae Ceaucescu's cult of personality had become unbearable. It was at the heart of the unraveling of power. Political blindness, ignorance and even stupidity, an immense vanity, his arbitrariness, despotism, and arrogant incompetence, when added to the dogmas and practices of a system already at the breaking point, transformed the personal control of power into a deplorable parody and a source of monumental blunders.

I dare to believe that had the country had the chance to be governed in a different manner, and if reason had managed to contain the dictatorship's excesses, even in a regime where reality contradicted the proclaimed ideals, Romania would have had a different face because of all its resources, especially its people, with their considerable intellectual level. Well, it was precisely the people and their abilities which were despised, their efforts made useless, their hopes disappointed. We must not forget that at the time and under similar conditions, other Central and Eastern European countries not any less "socialist" than we had achieved more promising and encouraging results, enabling them to evolve in a more balanced manner and keeping their chances for the future.

If in the mid-1960's Romania enjoyed a time of openness and hope, in a kind of avant-garde for southeastern Europe, ten years later it was on the road to becoming a

Stalinist bastion endowed with a particularly absurd and rigid political regime. Romania was a "block" within the Eastern European communist block, an island of immobility, more and more isolated from an evolving world asking itself fundamental questions about individuals' rights and freedoms. But a dictator remains generally unconvinced by the signs of History.

The foreign isolationism was as complete as the feeling of general paralysis within the country. The President and his wife found themselves more and more isolated, even from their cronies. The economic disaster was clear to everyone, beginning with those masking reality in order not to attract the dictator's disfavor. The daily difficulties of life had become unbearable for the near totality of a population, exasperated by food shortages, the cold of winter, the regular cuts in electricity, etc. (The list would be too long; others have already spoken about it.) Finally, the collapse of communism in neighboring countries, all with Moscow's consent, had aroused great hope and left no doubt as to the fate of a dictatorship whose longevity and absurdity had pushed the people to the brink. After the Hungarian, Czech, and Polish experiences, no popular uprising stood a chance of succeeding as long as the Red Army was there to defend the conquests of Socialism.

Heading a country which he believed supported him entirely, the president and his wife no longer had at their disposal any political base likely to support them. By broadening its reach to cover all of society, the Communist Party – 4 million members in a country of 22 million inhabitants, practically one Communist Party member per family – was no longer even the instrument of a minority capable of defending its privileges tooth and nail, but the extension of a personal dictatorship. At the time of the Revolution, this party which seemed to have merged with the State disappeared as a political power from one day to the next.

The excesses of this cult of personality had given rise to doubts even among the most opportunistic. No one seemed prepared to defend the regime, even if, at least within the scope of the system, no one seemed ready to risk contesting it. For a long time, disappointed by a power that claimed to be on their side and confronted with insurmountable financial difficulties, the workers rose up on several occasions, notably the Brasov factory uprisings and those of the Jiu Valley miners, to protest both against the economic policies responsible for their misery and against a dictatorship which seemed to no longer take their problems into consideration. In the event of an uprising, they would certainly make up the bulk of the troops. Exiled since the beginning of the "popular democracy" regime which exploited them in the name of industry's "socialist accumulation," the last few remaining peasants were also hoping for the fall of a regime which had left them nothing.

Isolated in libraries, universities and research centers, and convinced that this could not go on forever, intellectuals were also keeping alive the seed of hope for change. Without being able to openly protest against the regime but not willing to spare it either, they succeeded under often untenable working conditions to create a formidable counter-culture and to produce works of exceptional quality. They knew that they might face censorship.

Astonishingly absurd, this censorship did not succeed in blocking everything and authentic values managed to be affirmed, slowly and surreptitiously changing the people's psychology and their spiritual vision. This counter-culture's resistance contributed to the development of critical consciousness and destroyed, little by little, the mental supports of the regime. The day when it will be possible for us to peacefully examine these past years, undoubtedly, someone will write an alternative history of that time relating how a stifling and seemingly never-ending dictatorship smothered the country and how these intellectuals strengthened cultural creativity and its social audience. The people's dynamic energy, which could not assert itself because of the political situation, found compensation in masked cultural activities where they took their revenge on miserable historical circumstances by ruthlessly x-raying the communist regime. Using parables and allusive language which enabled them to confront what was forbidden by a regime which refused to look reality in the face, these truly heroic artists created an impressionistic painting of the drama we were living. They prepared our mindsets for the changes to come. For this they earned considerable prestige within a particularly vast and open social field.

The dissolution of totalitarian power cannot be understood if we do not take into consideration this counter-culture's reform action, a real attempt which defied the official propaganda and paved the spiritual path to change. Robbed of all freedom of thought and creativity but without ever losing their lucidity, intellectuals defied authority and called it into question more or less openly, weaving an account of the revolt which maintained and gave form to the entire country's resentments.

In addition, the dictatorship found itself confronted with the natural evolution of generations unfavorable to its causes. In twenty-five years, society's cultural outlook was considerably different and Nicolae Ceaucescu could no longer count on an older class of society which came of age during the Stalin years, educated in the spirit of the dictatorship of the proletariat and the cold war. Not to mention that he himself had become another person altogether, age having only aggravated his faults. Little by little, the gap between the dictator and the social reality had widened to become a chasm.

Isolated, commanding a nation that he did not understand anymore, Ceaucescu no longer had the means with which to perceive the new social sensibility. He was aware of this danger in 1971 when he dismissed from power all those who expressed this sensibility of renewal, myself among them. Far from being avoided, the danger became more and more threatening to those who were in power and forced them to acknowledge that the new Party officers had other intellectual agendas, other values and other hopes. The party was forced to became more open to intellectuals, to top-level specialists and to people of exceptional professional abilities who naturally ended up taking on responsibilities within the system. Although the Party system and its intellectual structure had profoundly changed, at the very top nothing happened.

Finally, the Party was no longer able to control the evolution of ideas within its own ranks. The people had different opinions than the ones they had been told to have and submitted to the ritual of offical remarks without believing a single treacherous word. Few in number, this fringe of new men took on Party responsibilities and enjoyed a growing influence on society's general development. At that point, Romanian society was destabilized by the enormous difference between every day reality and the ideological image of reality, by the difficulties of daily life (especially after Ceaucescu's decision to pay off the foreign debt immediately and at all costs), by several absurd bans and by political ossification which impeded all attempts to renew and reform a regime deaf to social demands and incapable of perceiving to what degree the ideological environment had changed. The dictator found himself alone and without any remaining support when the popular revolt came to chase him out.

Ceaucescu believed he could rally the people to defend him against all protests under the guise of patriotism, to make the public believe that the protests were a foreign manipulation. This did not make sense to me considering that other Eastern block countries, especially the Soviet Union, offered liberties that Romanians coveted. His policies went against the collective interest and the ideals of nationalism which are essential for a people's identity. Ceaucescu wanted to use these ideals for his own benefit; instead, he compromised them through his demagogic and superficial use, through fanaticism and grandiloquence.

Within the State bureaucracy, the army and even the police, dissatisfaction and incertitude regarding the future (including their own after the seemingly imminent political changes) were such that it appeared possible to overthrow a power which seemed to be hanging on by only a thread. The trust that many people had had in me since 1971 when I was first began to oppose the regime's drift (I had contacts with important State officials and could also count on support from a large part of the population due to being well enough known throughout the country) made me determined to search for political terms likely to be the foundations for democracy while at the same time sparing us the suffering of a revolution, like what occured in the other Soviet Block countries. Unfortunately, I did not succeed. No one could have. The armor of the dictatorship was too strong and those at the head of the Party were unwilling to undertake such a step. Nevertheless, I knew that the power was fragile, without any visible support, and that everything was at the breaking point. This explains the near instantaneous collapse of the regime under the blow of the popular uprising begun in Timisoara on the December, 16, 1989 and which continued the December, 21 and 22 in Bucharest and in other cities, especially Arad, Cluj, Sibiu and Brasov.

Almost an Ordinary Biography

Seen from the outside, it is probably difficult to understand my own evolution and that of my generation without a few explanations, even a summary, on the historical context and on the relations with the overthrown regime by the Revolution. Without giving more details than necessary, I believe that to have an accurate idea of what we are today, and what became of the 4 million Party members who in December 1989 did not opt for the mere eviction of a dictator but rather for a radical political change, we have to be able to understand the development of Romanian society, of which my experiences may be considered meaningful.

Dedicated communists, my parents suffered not only the persecution of Romania's authoritarian regime during the war years, but more surprisingly, also at the hands of their comrades.

The first and only one in his family to continue beyond elementary school, at the School of Arts and Trades of his native town, my father was a locomotive mechanic who worked in the Bucharest railroad workshops. He joined the union movement and in a completely natural manner, joined the outlawed Communist Party. Arrested in 1939 for his political activities, he was interned in 1940 in a camp where he met Gheourghiu-Dej, who became the absolute ruler of Romania a few years later, the unwavering secretary-general of the Communist Party who my father saw rise to power in 1945 and who held power until he died in 1964. My father, who had considerable prestige within the workers' movement, contested the authoritarian manner in which Gheorghiu-Dej's staff settled Party business. At the 5th Party Congress, my father had blamed its leaders for neglecting the workers' concrete, immediate and legitimate demands. He had also expressed doubts about the Resolution adopted on that occasion concerning the problems of ethnicities[1], which appeared to him to be the result of an analysis ignoring reality and national interests. These opinions earned him some people's hostility. He was expelled from the Party while he was in prison and died in

1945 at the age of 44, shortly after being released. For re-fusing to leave her banished husband once he left prison, my mother was also expelled. Gheorghiu-Dej was still holding a grudge twelve years later in 1957. In a private conversation I had with him, the First Secretary of the Romanian C.P. was still justifying the measures taken against my parents.

In spite of these "accidents" which marked my childhood and adolescence, I spent the first sixteen years of my life fueled by the idea that communism was going to bring happiness to the humble and would give them back their dignity. All around me, new political forces seemed to be most concerned with liquidating the after-effects of fas-cism (my father had been one of its numerous victims) and with re-establishing democracy. In that respect, these forces appeared to me to be supported, especially in Europe, by a movement bringing together the most presti-gious names: political and cultural personalities whose au-thority reassured us and led us to believe that against all opposition, we were on the side of the forces of progress, the side which was preparing humanity's radiant future. Raised in a house with a dirt floor, the fact that I was able to enroll at the Polytechnic Institute and to live in a little bit less miserable surroundings seemed sufficient for me to believe that we were on the right track.

---

1. The 5th Congress of the Romanian Communist Party, though forbidden, took place in 1931. As a final resolution, it put forth theses without any foundation for the Komintern, ac-cording to which Romania – united national State which had acquired its present borders in 1918 from the Union who freely gave the regions to Romania up until the time of the Austro-Hungarian empire and the tsar – was an "imperialist" State. This resolution asked the Communist Party to fight against "imperialism" in order to defend "the right of oppressed nations to self-determination and to separate from the Romanian State." These theses denied the historic reality of the unity of the Romanian State and placed the Romanian Communist Party in a position which went against national interests.

In those years after the war, our generation which had known the horrors of war and had been confronted by fascism, was hoping for a more just and open democracy, to spare future generations the trials that we had just suffered. Who can blame us for having believed this? Lacking political experience, still not having suffered History's hard lessons and ignorant of how the world was divided up at Yalta, we were convinced that the Soviet occupation was temporary and that life would soon go back to normal. We never could have imagined that Romania was going to be cut off from Europe, which it had always been a part of. At that time, who could have foreseen the coming atrocities? Just like Soviet citizens themselves, we had no idea of the Stalinist terror in the Soviet Union, and we were completely unaware of the repression that was raging within our own country. The elimination of certain traditional parties from our political life, even the liquidation of certain "parasitic classes" through the abolition of giant properties and the nationalization of industry seemed natural to me in so far as they were forces hostile to the construction of this new society, a hopefully more just and equitable one. The industrialization and "socialist" accumulation programs seemed necessary to me to do away with the economic backwardness and to modernize the country. The accumulation of capital, a necessary condition for industrial expansion, had been done in the West in worse conditions throughout several centuries: the brutal exploitation of workers had been more ruthless than in our country, where the power structure seemed concerned with maintaining a social justice which was supposed to assure the State's fundamental balances.

I was 16-17 years old when I enlisted in a student democratic movement, 19 when I entered the Bucharest Polytechnical Institute, 20 in 1950 when I left for Moscow to study at the world-renowned Energy Studies Institute.

It was there, when I saw Soviet reality, perhaps also losing adolescent naïvety along the way, that I started to doubt not the system in general but what it had become in the Soviet Union. Some of my Soviet friends and their families, who belonged to the USSR's various peoples, were poor and lived in shabby conditions. Consequences of war, I said to myself – I was disappointed by the living conditions which were so different than the image which they wanted to portray to us. The people were wary not only of foreigners but also of anything that came from outside the country; it was shocking for a communist Romanian who was living there after the war and who was curious about what went on elsewhere. Like the interior passport which prohibited travel within the country without alerting the police. There was also the ubiquitous political police, who my friends feared, only daring to say what they thought in whispers and in lowered voices. And then, the displays of despair at Stalin's death! What was this political system capable of creating new gods? Returning to Romania to work as a hydro-energy engineer (in a great project to evaluate the country's hydro-energy resources), I was chosen to represent Romania at the World Student Organization. Then, in 1956, I organized a Romanian students association, hoping to not only give students a tool to improve their lives, but also a place where they could meet and exchange ideas. This activity allowed me to travel, to see Western countries, and to meet openly with other students, left-wing people who dared to ask themselves questions that I still did not have the courage to ask or the chance to confront. They opened new horizons for me, they made me discover another way of looking at the world, they gave me reference points that I did not have before. One morning at the UNEF Congress in Strasbourg and after conversations had brought us together, Marco Pannella, president of an Italian student association who would later become an important politician in his country, brought me the newspaper "Le Monde" which had published extracts of Khrushchev's report at the 20th Congress of the Soviet Communist Party concerning Stalin's crimes.

It was a political and intellectual watershed. As far as I was concerned, it had come just in time: at 20 years old, you have faith, at 26 years old, you are ready to no longer believe blindly. I discovered the works of Trotsky, Boukharine and Roy Medvedev; I found texts about the Soviet Union by Panaït Istrati and by André Gide. I read a good amount of political analyses calling the Soviet system into question, sometimes submitting the system to a Marxist critique in order to conclude that it had been delinquent, sometimes contesting its political and economic choices on principles, that while not appearing indisputable, nonetheless made puzzling contradictions arise between theory and Soviet practice, between Utopian ambitions and every day reality. In the evolution towards democratic convictions and towards a new way of thinking, those of us who sincerely believed that scientific communism's fundamental ideas were the most profound and humanistic were forced to recognize the Soviet model's failure for the first time. This was the "childhood illness" of my generation.

My career in the Party system corresponds to a larger political development which was arousing hopes. The 20th Congress of the Soviet Communist Party made more balanced relationships possible between communist parties in which the right to independently establish political beliefs in keeping with national realities was clearly recognized. This opened the door to a national communism which we hoped would be a new version, stripped of the corruption which had made the Soviet Union a totalitarian country. Following smart negotiations between Romanian leaders and Khruschev, in 1958, the Soviet armies left Romania. During 1963 and 1964, Romania rejected Khruschev's plan to integrate the Eastern Block countries into economic structures without linking them to national borders – an indirect way to reinforce Soviet supremacy and the enslavement of the "socialist" countries to the interests of the "big brother." The debate which followed this questioned the relationship with the Soviet Union and at the same time gave rise to the idea of a national economic model, which, for the first time, was conceived differently than the Soviet model.

In 1964, all political prisoners were released. At the same time, the Party had sufficiently changed and opened up so that in 1965, a large number of intellectuals joined. Nicolae Ceaucescu seemed determined to change the Party's political slant by ending once and for all Stalinism's aftereffects and by rehabilitating its victims and those marginalized and persecuted during this period. In 1967, an important national Party conference accepted the principle of a market economy and recognized the necessity of steering the Romanian economy towards modernization, taking into account the law of supply and demand as it is explicitly recognized to function even in a socialist economy, although in a specific manner. This created a period of political and intellectual openness toward the West which was accompanied by economic, technological, scientific and artistic exchanges of particular benefit to our country. At this time, Romania was the "avant-garde" of the socialist bloc, sufficiently free from Soviet guardianship to dare to implement a series of measures to renovate the system. Finally, in August 1968, when Romania refused to lend its armies to crush the Prague Spring and "socialism with a human face," a national consensus was formed around the Romanian Communist Party and its leaders[1].

During these years, in public meetings and in the workplace, I met tens of thousands of people to whom I always listened with much attention, trying to understand their problems. I knew the workings and weaknesses of the system. I told them my doubts and the people began to trust me because what I was telling them corresponded with what they themselves thought. They saw in me a man who desired to serve in a politically fair and equitable manner, able to offer tools compatible with the dignity of all to the ideals of social justice. That I would give everyone the chance to affirm his personality, favoring the open discus-

---

1. I myself had the opportunity to condemn the Soviet invasion of Czechoslovakia on August 22, 1968 in a speech given at the National Assembly as a representative leader of youth. I said that "nothing justifies the military occupation of Czechoslovakia; it is unacceptable," that "this invasion constitutes a serious violation of the most basic norms of elementary international law", and that "those who took the initiative and carried out this military intervention are guilty of grave mistake toward their own people and all of humanity. The Czechoslovakian military intervention is an absurd act which will leave a deep wound on the conscience of humanity."

sion of ideas, open to all logical arguments preceded by correct reasoning. That I would assess people according to the principles of social justice and loyalty, according to their competence, their moral conduct and their public-spiritedness, under the banner of a democratic relationship between citizens having the right to express their opinions. I can genuinely say that my moral authority and popularity today are largely due to the rectitude and honesty which I proved to possess, even during the most difficult moments of the period which we have just lived through.

But the radical change in my political beliefs was due to the political experience I acquired little by little within the Party system itself, and not only to my way of thinking, but to my entire cultural environment. After having had my doubts about the Soviet system, I lost faith in the system altogether when the encouraging changes in Romanian society were brutally halted by the installation of Nicolae Ceaucescu's personal dictatorship. He was not the only person at fault. Narrow-minded and uncultivated, Nicolae Ceaucescu was part of a circle that did not understand that a politician's competence is not the sum of specifically learned ideas of all of those whose interests he takes charge- without going so far as believing, like Raymond Aron, that democracy is a regime of experts led by amateurs. Why not admit that we are forced to make decisions according to advice that people give us, who are each more competent in their field than we could ever be? Victim to an illusion that he himself had adjusted the system for political reasons, Nicolae Ceaucescu ended up getting caught in his own trap and sincerely believed that he was more of an engineer than the engineers, more of an artist than the artists and more of a worker than the workers. In fact, what bothered me even more was the political mechanism which had enabled such an unrefined politican to seize power, to block the system's development and, finally, to corrupt the meaning and function of the State.

My own spiritual development was now going to go through a more radical stage. I was making a lucid comparison of the Communist experience with the general development of contemporary civilization. The conclusion was traumautic: the human price for its modest technological and economic performances was disproportionate. The centralized planned economy led to pernicious deadlocks, and our society's potential development remained largely untapped. Individual freedoms had been suppressed and individual property outlawed. Intellectual vigor and individual talents languished in a void, while critical thought and the natural outlets for opposition and social dialogue had been completely stifled. In short, this system was producing monsters even while it seemed to be improving: the dictatorships that it brought about were not just coincidence but the inevitable outcome of an unnatural political institution which could only work by suppressing pluralism and diversity, democratic processes, and the collective and individual freedoms of all.

This experience convinced me that if a regime does not allow its citizens to freely express their political and social opinions, if it does not provide them with the means to censure the power structure through free elections, and if it does not allow everyone's ideas and choices to be heard and confronted within the framework of democratic debate, then this system is incapable of correcting its errors, of insuring society's smooth operation and of adapting itself to the demands of contemporary development. Yet it was clear that the regime as it existed excluded political pluralism, democratic freedoms for individuals, the elementary right to think and to offer alternative solutions. The intellectual split was violent and I often found myself torn by deeply upsetting personal dilemmas. What could we do? Could the system be restructured and still keep its institutional and political framework? Or did we have to abandon it completely? Very dramatic and troubling questions. It was impossible for us to envision radical solutions because no one foresaw the geopolitical upheavals of the last years. We were stuck in the deep freeze of the Cold War and nothing led us to believe that the Iron Curtain would one day disappear.

I was not the only one to confront myself with these questions. Indeed, given the political climate at the time, everyone had this kind of personal dialogue; it was a very personal self-examination that we undertook at our own risk. Also at our own risk were the attitudes that we could take in our daily lives. I noticed just how right Marx was in stressing the importance of barriers devised by the Paris Commune (eligibility requirements for the civil servants, term limits, a balanced budget), to prevent the State's pernicious drift noticeable in Romanian political life. I do not doubt that today certain polemicists will smile when reading a remark invoking such a source, but I recall that at the time these works that we were happy to cite in our country were considered authoritative among the most reputable Western intellectuals.

Without forgetting that in the 1960's and '70's, the most enterprising political thought was not centered in the Eastern block countries but rather in the West, where the European Left, endowed with great diversity and political figures in the foreground, observed with detachment but with precision and objectivity the practices of "socialist" countries and brought new ideas and plans forbidden to us. Theories concerning the "the convergence of systems","post-industrial societies", "technocracy", or even "unity in diversity", and later "Eurocommunism" were bridges which, despite their weak practical efficiency, offered us meeting points, questioned us, and rallied us to the common will for change and for the construction of a new kind of society. Despite its origin and its political motivation, this intellectual movement made us think and made us look with greater attention and a more aroused critical spirit at our own reality.

Little by little, I started to suspect that the harm was due solely to the Party, which suppressed all social input to the political world and immediately dismissed any social criticism of power. At the same time, lacking true social feedback, the political authorities lost all contact with reality and entered into an utterly absurd process, their actions no longer responding to real needs but to ideological fantasies.

Clearly, it was not enough to reform the Party. The debate had to be opened up to all of the nation's political forces to allow ideas to be expressed within the system and to enable them to form as elements of power. This is indispensible in order for those in power to remain connected with reality.

In 1971, while on a trip to Asia, I expressed my doubts about North Korea's totalitarian and dehumanizing system which had transformed its citizens into robots incapable of thinking for themselves or at least forbade them to say what they truly thought to an enthusiastic Nicolae Ceaucescu. Then, when we got back, I confronted him at a meeting about the activities of Party officers, trying to get him to accept the idea that concerning the orientation of general policies, responsiblities are collective and instead of looking for individual responsiblities, it would be more useful to examine the Party's operation and its institutions. I knew that he would not tolerate such a defiance. I acted in response to a fundamental political conviction; it would henceforth be impossible for me to approve of and participate in a dictatorship's upper-level management which was leading the country to disaster. I was immediately accused of "intellectual deviation." A discussion to explain to me what this term meant never took place and I did not investigate further the reasons for my dismissal since the reasons were clear to me.

I was dismissed from power (sent to Timisoara as secretary of propaganda), then given a second chance (first secretary of the Iasi department), then sent to a dead-end job (president of the National Water Council) and finally politically buried (director of Technical publications). This did not stop me from continuing to openly speak my mind[1] – taking advantage, it's true, of the prestige I had gained and which prevented Ceaucescu from eliminating me for fear of provoking turmoil that he considered wise to avoid. Moreover, in 1969 the Party had rehabilitated the victims of Romanian Stalinism with much ceremony, among them my father. Realizing that comparisons could have been made, it would not have been wise to sack the son of a man rehabilitated for having suffered precisely the same kind of abuse. It is also necessary to add that foreign radio stations, firstly "Free Europe," were echoing my position, which led him to believe that sanctions against me would not go unnoticed.

I was isolated, it's true, and since 1971, under continuous surveillance. My telephone was tapped. Reliable sources have told me that micophones were placed in my office. And for a long time, I was continually followed by two or three cars which were in no way trying to conceal themselves. This considerably reduced my contacts with people, some of whom were openly discouraged to contact me and others who, without having to be told, were aware of the risk involved in seeing me. This did not stop others from taking advantage of the smallest occasion, under professional pretexts, at the publishing house where I worked, or in private, to meet me and to let me know that I could count on them.

---

1. It is perhaps useful to recall some of the positions I took demonstrating the continuity of my political thought, which did not just change over-night at the moment of the December 1989 Revolution:

- My intervention at the June 1976 "Congress of political education and socialist culture" (which was the last time I participated in a national forum). I condemned "triumphalism, apology, festivism and abstract idealism"; I spoke out equally severely against bureaucracy and social parasitism; I affirmed as well that "our people do not judge others by their words, but by their actions... He who speaks about principles in which he himself does not believe cannot hope to be respected, just as we scoff at the vain who preach modesty, those who talk about dignity and courage without practicing these things themselves, those who give lessons in morality when they have no morals themselves and those who speak for the cause of democracy and show themselves to be ignorant." Transparent and clear-cut, these statements were coldly greeted by the presidium, but welcomed with warm applause by the audience;

- The series of articles published between 1980 and 1984 concerning the problems of hydrology and ecology, which were in sharp contrast with the idyllic pictures painted by the system;

- The contradictory discussions undertaken during the same time-period with Nicolae

More numerous were those with whom I discussed (while walking in the street or in the park between my home and office) fundamental problems and the regime's corruption while devising political solutions and circumstances likely to allow us to break free of the deadlock.

In addition, I was disappointed by some of the personal contacts I had had with certain political leaders at the top of the pyramid, who carefully avoided all discussion about possible changes and did not leave me with any hope for their abilities to bring about the needed renewal that everyone was calling for, incapable as they were to undertake the risks of such an enterprise.

Indeed, during this period numerous other initiatives cropped up, individual or in small groups – such as a letter written by six former communist leaders[2] – explosions of

Ceaucescu on the subect of certain abberant hydro-energy projects (especially the Danube-Black Sea Canal which was extremely costly, had no economic justifications and was particularly harmful to the Arges' minor streams and to the surrounding environment); This ended in my dismissal from the post of President of the National Water Council;

- The report published in 1985 by Political Publishing titled "Contemporary Development and the Role of Power Factors" in which, concerning the world crisis and the evolution of contemporary society, I brought up the way in which "the power factors can stimulate development, but also can hold it back and can retard social renewal." I pointed out the wide variety of socio-economic conditions in contemporary society, and after having condemned those who did not manage to understand this and who refused to take the diverse and often opposing opinions and interests of different communities into account, examined the ties which link democracy and development today and the fact that it is impossible to evolve if we do not give people the chance to participate in fundamental social decisions. I demonstrated to what point the contempt for diverse opposing views of different communities is harmful to general development and I concluded by underlining "the necessity to democratize the political world and to broaden the forms of social influence on those in charge of making political decisions;"

- The article published in 1988 in the magazine "România Literara," titled "Creation and Information," about the role of intellectual creation and technological and scientific progress in contemporary society. One sentence stands out where I quoted Francis Bacon as saying "knowledge signifies power." I followed this by saying that the opposite is not true, which was interpreted as an allusion to the absurd efforts of the President and his wife, especially Elena Ceaucescu, to pass as cultured people. Once again, the question was about the need to exert social influence on a power which, in defending order and the status quo, stood the risk of appearing as a force of inertia, likely to provoke a very dangerous social alienation.

discontent here and there, in the carbon mines or in the Brasov enterprises, but these isolated incidents were not enough to put the dictatorship in danger. At the beginning of 1989, I became convinced that lacking politicians or superior officers capable of taking the initiative, of isolating Ceaucescu and of carrying out a velvet revolution, like those recently happening in other Communist block countries, Romania could only count on a popular uprising.

In 1989, for a great number of people, I was someone who had believed just like them in a socialist society and who had turned away from it; I had proved it by leaving the national leadership and making no move to return to it during the twenty years since my dismissal.

If the December Revolution – unlikely in 1971 when I left power, unforeseeable (at that point) in the long run, and for which it would be absurd to believe that I had prepared myself – entrusted me with highly important responsibilities. I believe that this is also due to the fact that my personal experience had been that of an entire generation which had had to renounce utopias to rediscover the natural values of democracy.

Those who want to believe in a conspiracy at all costs and against all evidence are wrongly giving me credit – immediately qualified as conspiracy – for the Timisoara uprising, where it's true that I knew a lot of people since I had worked there. Moreover, beginning on December 20, the demonstrators were proclaiming my name in the streets.

---

2. It was an open letter signed by six people who had held important positions within the Party and government and who were protesting Nicolae Ceaucescu's dictatorship; The letter was broadcast on Radio Free Europe, the BBC and Radio Liberty. The six people were Silviu Brucan, Constantin Pârvulescu (who had already questioned Nicolae Ceaucescu's policies at the 12th Congress of the Romanian Communist Party in 1979), Alexandru Bârladeanu and Corneliu Manescu (former Minister of Foreign Affairs).

I would be proud to have been able to provoke the Timisoara uprising, or the Bucharest uprising, but this is not the case.

The Timisoara Uprising

A spark was all that was needed for the general discontent to explode. I was mindful of the political meaning of the events and of the sociological root causes that manifested themselves in the December 1989 movement and for which the new power had to find a solution. I did not let myself be carried away into the controversy about economic reasons having provoked the Timisoara uprising, especially the idea that it could have been provoked by a foreign power.

Clearly for specific reasons but also with a viewpoint for the total development of Eastern Europe, our neighbors (notably the USSR and Hungary) were hoping for Nicolae Ceaucescu's fall, without really having the means to provoke it. Uncomfortable for having supported at arm's length for so long this particularly foul regime, the West appeared ready to make amends. The West contented itself with encouraging a few dissidents with the hope that they would turn from a purely intellectual challenge to the regime to a complete political opposition.

Where were these people when the events erupted? It's a difficult question to answer. I myself do not have facts at my disposal which would allow me to be certain about it. Following up this kind of intervention falls under the jurisdiction of the intelligence services of the Securitatea, which, from the beginning of fall and especially starting in December, collected conclusive proof of intensified foreign activity but which may have fabricated some of it to lend credence to Ceaucescu's theory that he was threatened by an international conspiracy. Afterwards, investigations could not dismiss the theory of foreign intervention, without really presenting irrefutable proof confirming it.

Quickly overrun by the magnitude of the street demonstrations, the intelligence officers dispatched to Timisoara were no longer in a position to fulfill their task, still less in the days that followed the dictatorship's fall. Immediately placed under army control with its equipment, the Securitatea and its intelligence branch no longer existed. Its officers, including those of its intelligence branch were arrested while waiting for justice to fully determine each person's responsibility in the repression.

Today certain people reproach those who, at that time, found themselves at the head of Council for the National Salvation Front for having abolished the Securitatea, whose control the army took over the night of December 22 to the 23, thus leaving the country defenseless at a time when the open borders would considerably ease the actions of foreign intelligence services. This is not a baseless remark. Nevertheless we have to take into consideration the extraordinary popular pressure which wanted the immediate destruction of the structures of the former regime and especially its instruments of repression – the Securitatea first of all, which was especially detested by all of the citizens. Others are convinced that the Securitatea still exists, or at least that it keeps some of its structures and that its officers continue to spy on Romanian society.

This is a completely ludicrous idea, about which I will talk more in depth about it at the right time.

I prefer to examine the question carefully in order to hold on to the conclusions which seem logical to me, and for lack of certainty, I limit myself to what seems reasonable to me. It goes without saying that under such circumstamces, all the special services of countries having interests in that area had sent agents to the scene. The Securitatea's reports were not detailed, generally treating them as hostile elements or as enemies of the socialist State. It is, thus, difficult to be informed about facts and to distinguish those who had precise missions of diversion or provocation from those who had been sent to obtain reliable information needed by their governments, journalists who had smelled out a scoop or simply good-will ambassadors coming to give their personal support to threatened dissidents. But it has been established that around mid-December, the number of Soviet and Hungarian "tourists" travelling for personal reasons by car or by bus had considerably risen, to the point where those in charge of keeping an eye on them no longer could.

The atmosphere was very tense and everyone was waiting for a change that could wait no more. The fall of the Berlin Wall, "the velvet revolution" in Czechoslovakia, and also to a certain extent in Bulgaria, the troubles in East Germany, where they were already talking about reunification – all of this under the eye of a newly consenting Moscow that watched the fall of all of these regimes without blinking – had surprised the entire world and most especially the West. Obviously, it would not be long before Romania took the same track – it was bound to happen sooner or later.

Notorious for being the last European bastion of hardline Soviet communism, Nicolae Ceaucescu's Romania was in the international limelight. The desire to directly aid in the fall of a particularly detestable dictatorship sent us many journalists from all over the world and without a doubt, quite a few foreign agents ready to destabilize those in power (which implied enormous risks for a result that would occur anyway) or to at least help those who were likely to take action.

Whatever the hypotheses and different versions of the story which have and continue to circulate may be, I remain convinced that foreign interference had only a secondary role in triggering off the Timisoara popular uprising. This time defying repression, the people were determined and had the courage and the valor to so substantially revolt that the entire country noticed it and saw the opportunity to fearlessly protest. In fact, what prolonged Ceaucescu's regime was not so much the repression itself but rather the absolute control of information. Each time that a demonstration sprang up somewhere, it was extinguished before other hotbeds of revolt could learn about it and flare up themselves. In order to lead to a significant political result, several explosions had to take place at the same time. Therefore, the State system very efficiently withheld all communication and all discussions likely to lead to what we call a "mass effect." The importance of the Timisoara events comes from the fact that the people held out long enough for this mass effect to occur. Especially with the Bucharest protest, where the people knew that their protest was adding to that of the one still raging at Timisoara and were sure that people elsewhere would follow in their footsteps.

It is always tempting to speculate and understandable to a certain point. Revolutions have always given rise to legends. They feed the imagination and generate fantastic interpretations, as with the story of Reverend Tokes. Today, everyone knows him and knows about his feats and actions. But at the time, he enjoyed a considerable aura thanks to some people's assiduousness who immediately made a hero out of him and who suceeded in the confusion to impose the false image of one man alone being capable of unleashing the Timisoara events. In fact, he had been transferred to another parish in the region, and was consequently asked to leave the parish apartment that he lived in. He refused, in spite of a court decision. This was on December 15. Surrounded by several faithful colleagues who supported him, Reverend Tokes ended up confronting the police who were sent to evict him. That would be it if not for the fact that at the same exact moment – by chance or coincidence, by signal or because it was an opportunity to grab – the entire population of Timisoara was set into motion. But it is unrealistic to believe that a movement of such a magnitude, which then spread to the rest of the country, can be explained by this young man's personal affair, a very diligent and active clergyman, but completely obscure up until that time. Nevertheless, this idea got around and certain people believe it even today. My opinion is that it was a totally insignificant episode. When a piece of cloth is rotting, the smallest little thorn can tear it, and politically, it is not this tiny snag that counts, but the long process of the material's deterioration. The Romanian social material was in a state of decomposition and was releasing a force whose meaning it was necessary to understand and for which it was necessary to provide the tools of power to it.

I did not have the least doubt that the protests against the dictatorship were just the tip of the iceberg and that the popular uprising wanted the end of a communist system in which no one believed. This desire seemed sufficiently simple and clear to cut across all social groups, all layers of the population and to also bring in the army and a part of the police. Nicolae Ceaucescu's defenders were not legion and I was convinced that if they took up arms, they would only do so to escape from serious sanctions in the unfortunate case of the revolution's failure.

The danger was that a too violent explosion, which would transform their frustrations into a murderous settling of old scores whose principal victims would be the Party leaders and the police, could force them to reflexively defend themselves. We had to avoid this at all costs because it could set off a civil war with immesurable consequences.

I got wind of what was happenning in Timisoara on December 17 through one of my employees. Our publishing house was working with ten or so printers spread throughout the country and, notably, with one in Timisoara. While he was following up on one of our publications, one of my editors had spoken on the telephone, just before losing the connection, with our printer in Timisoara. He let it be known, in not so many words but with great emotion, that things were happenning over there. Extremely troubled, he immediately came to talk to me about it, not so much to inform me that something was out of the ordinary but to show sympathy and solidarity in keeping with the political positions that I had always defended.

It was the long awaited uprising. I was sure of it. I was convinced that the army hierarchy and the police, more fearful of their fate under a foreseen political change than of the sanctions of a dying regime, would falter and that this sentiment would be passed down to the troops, who would refuse to particpate in a bloody repression and would side with the protesters. And that is exactly what happenned in Timisoara on December 20. All the pieces of the revolutionary machine seemed to be in place and only political action could avoid and spare the country of its convulsions. Unfortunately, those who were in a position to do something about it were so compromised and reviled that they could not hope for any leniency once the Ceaucescu dictatorship was overthrown.

As for me, lacking all tools allowing me to take effective action, too removed from the decision-making center to be able to construct something coherent that would lead to Ceaucescu's fall, trailed by security agents whose complicity I could not count on and who could have arrested me, I still had to wait.

The Time to Act

C eaucescu's call for a massive rally in Bucharest surprised me. It proved to what extent he was unaware of the country's reality, not having the slightest idea about the social tensions and the feelings of those he was asking for support. The population's hatred for him became still more violent upon learning of the bloody repression of the

Timisoara demonstrations. It was an act of suicide and in fact it detonated the general movement that swept him away. Jeering interrupted his speech. Thanks to live TV, which broadcast it nationally, the entire country witnessed this defiance. The people of Bucharest were set in motion and several other cities followed suit.

That December 21, I left the technical publishers, the three police cars still on my heels. In the evening, I was updated on the demonstrations that had taken place in the city and then we heard the first gunshots. Army units, deployed here and there, appeared sometimes idle, sometimes ready to join in with the crowd. This confirmed my analysis of the situation.

The next morning, when I left for work, the three police cars were still there. The people were in a state of excitement nearing the explosion point. Through my office window, I saw columns of demonstrators who had come in from working-class suburbs and were heading downtown. I went down to another office where people were watching television. Apparently, immense crowds were spilling out into the streets of Bucharest and had tried to enter the Central Committee building.

I went back to my office, gathered my belongings and left the publishing house. The police cars had disappeared. With a handful of colleagues from work who wanted to see what was going to happen, we headed toward the television headquarters.

I had the feeling that we were living one of those rare moments where History was in the making. Unlike a coup d'etat or a more or less planned revolution where the political forces were precisely aware of their objectives and prepared for that event, our revolution left us not knowing where the pieces of the new power were going to land, which political winds would have the chance to assume positions in the new government, and even less sure which figures would have the chance to rise to this new power from the energy released from this immense explosion. In a situation like this, full of danger and hope, certain people chose to lock themselves up in their houses, refusing to participate in this perilous game, fearful of finding themselves spurned by History. Too concerned with their own pride, they prefer not to play the game than to wind up as losers. Others let themselves be caught up by the wave at all costs, with no other objective than to just be present during the events, which in any case chose on their own those whom they wanted to use and to give a historic mission to. The events chose them according to a logic which at that time escaped us, but which later during peace time, professors, researchers, and scientists demonstrated as being the only logical reasoning conceivable, surprised that we had not realized it earlier.

By deciding to go on television, I made a simple decision: to participate in the unfolding events and to attempt to be present where the most crucial developments concerning the country's future were happening. Frankly, in moments of insane enthusiasm when you lose all your fears, when the only thing that counts is to take part in this unique act, I let myself be carried away by the people's fervor, who felt like they were changing History. Faced with this gigantic release of energy, I told myself that the most urgent thing was to offer coherence to this massive spontaneous movement, to avoid chaos and anarchy and to form the seed for the new power. This seed had to be the magnet around which all factions could rally, to prevent this snowball from becoming an avalanche. But before becoming an avalanche you have to take the snow ball and roll it.

There was a large crowd in front of the television building. I was recognized and led to studio 4. I briefly saluted the popular movement and I appealed to all those capable to contribute in the foundation of a new government structure to come and meet me at 5 o'clock at the seat of the ex-Central Committee, the holy ground of the fallen power.

It was all the more urgent to do this as everything was in a state of total confusion. Among all those pushing and shoving to talk about the violence of the frustration and the enthusiasm of the liberation in front of the camera, no one seemed aware of the dangers facing the country, nor did they seem worried about the functioning of the State, nor did they seem to have the slightest idea what must be done or how to go about solving the general problems which were already beginning to crop up. In short, they did not know what power meant, how it was organized, how it worked, and about the tasks falling on those who assume responsibility. We were already beginning to feel (and not wrongly as we later proved!) the danger of chaos, total societal disorganization and anarchy. I told myself that we had to take care of it and I took the initiative, through the simple reflex of being a politician.

My first aim was to propose a program which would enable the regrouping of a reliable social force throughout the country. From that moment on, I defined several principles with extreme clarity: the liquidation of totalitarian State structures and their instrument, the Communist

Party, the installation of democracy and pluralism within a Constitutional State Lawful State system, free elections, respect of individual liberties, human rights and minority rights, and an opening towards the West and the transition into a market economy.

The idea of this appeal was perhaps not very apt; at five o'clock in the afternoon the grounds of the Central Committee were swarming with people. In the setting sun of the winter evening, their bulky clothing taking all identity away from them, the people who were shoving and pushing and whose eyes we could hardly see, were swept up by a contagious enthusiasm, its power difficult to describe, a sort of electricity that you could almost feel tingling on your skin and which made you think that charges were going to pass through your physical body. No single danger, no single warning could have kept this force from reacting to the slightest provocation. Never before had I so strongly felt the responsiblity which had befallen me, not only for the construction of a new power, but also to prevent the confrontations which could be terrible. I succeeded with much difficulty in clearing a path to one of the doors blocked by those who had already occupied the building, and who, after disarming the security officers in order to arm themselves, did not want to allow anyone into an already cramped space, to prevent any possible attempt to take back this symbolic place. It took a moment for those inside to realize who I was. They finally opened the door, letting in twenty or so individuals in with me who pushed through the gap. I was immediately led to the balcony by the actor Ion Caramitru and some other people. The people wanted to hear me speak from this grandstand which had become the temple of the Revolution and where orators had been speaking one after the other for hours. I took advantage of this opportunity to express several clear and simple political principles: the immediate organization of free elections, the democratization of the political world, the respect for human rights and fundamental liberties, and so on.

The most important thing was to draw up a program signed by those who had taken on the responsibility of the moment and to immediately distribute it so that a political force and structure of power could form around expressed ideas. To the detriment of all those, too numerous, who would have wanted to participate, we withdrew in a small group to outline the Call to the nation. There were people there who had only found a political calling on the occasion of the events that we were experiencing, Old Guard dissident communists, and strangers too. So we began by introducing ourselves! Then we got to the work of elaborating the Revolution's first document, of which I am perfectly aware today that no one else would have drawn up with the same terms. At that moment, it was clear to everyone that this revolution was not merely the rejection of a dictatorship but that of the entire system, and that what people were expecting from us was a program of radical reform setting up a modern democracy.

The First Gunshots

We had barely started drawing up the document when sometime around 6:30 PM and 7 PM the first gunshots were fired.

Our feeling was that they were firing from inside of the building itself, which was surprising since the occupants' first concern had been to disarm the security agents, who had offered no resistance whatsoever. It was a climate of panic and suspicion and of excitement and violence; people of all kinds, who found themselves with a weapon in their hands for the first time, and who were arresting and releasing each other inside the building itself, could easily have been the source of the gunfire.

I will get back to this later, but it is perhaps a good idea to mention right now that probably quite a few shootings were accidental, regrettable blunders which, in this state of confusion and excitement, aroused counter attacks, each taking the other for a supporter of the old regime, for a "terrorist" – this is the term the press used to describe these lone gunmen who spread panic for several days, especially in Bucharest. People saw these "terrorists" everywhere and sometimes in an excessive revolutionary fervor, sometimes in a vain and clumsy quest for heroism, or even acting out of panic, some of these gunmen killed innocent people, unnecessary victims of a situation impossible for us to control. Who were these "terrorists?"

It is difficult for me to be sure. Some files concerning this issue are in the authorities' competent hands in Bucharest, Sibiu, Brasov, and Timisoara, who, as far as I know, investigated the matter.

I took care not get involved in it, not wanting to overstep my authority, nor to once again ignite the feelings of an era where what we have principally obtained – and what seems to me is our principal achievement – is to have safeguarded civil order and peace in spite of the critical situations we have been through and the provocations we have had to face.

Filmmaker Sergiu Nicolaescu, one of the most important figures in the Revolution who is now a senator, has personally led extensive investigations, apparently without being able to get beyond simple suspicions, not having succeeded in supporting them with any hard proof. Today, another parliamentary commission, led by one of the principal opposition leaders, Senator Valentin Gabrielescu, has taken over the investigation.

The facts are all the more difficult to establish since the organization with the means to collect this kind of information, the Securitatea, has disappeared, abolished as an institution. Even worse, the arrests and interrogations of supposed terrorists were done in a completely haphazard manner by people who considered themselves investigators. Totally incompetent, these people were unable to collect hard evidence and create files which the authorities could then consider reliable. If the "real" terrorists were among the many innocent people arrested on these occasions, they had no problem making the proof disappear and being crafty enough to keep the authorities from getting their hands on any incriminating evidence within the confines of a legal investigation and a process of presumed innocence. In brief, the courts were not able to find anyone sufficiently guilty to convict them with the certainty that such a judgement demands. If some particularly scrupulous judges, respectful of the individual rights and liberties acquired by the Revolution let some criminals get away, I am grateful that they hesitated to convict innocent people. And in a democracy, this is what counts.

To conclude from this that there was no resistance is a step I will not take.

Those who accuse the new government and myself of having feigned the start of a civil war simply to strengthen our positions should, if not give some evidence of this – which would not be impossibe to come by – to at least explain what reasoning could lead to such a surprising attitude. At that time, no one challenged me personally nor did they challenge the Council for the National Salvation Front, which was the Revolution's political expression, nor the program which this council proposed to the country. With this new power immediately being in control of the army and the police, I have a hard time seeing why it would endanger itself by provoking troubles which could only serve to compromise an already acquired and unanimously recognized position.

As always, for lack of indisputable facts, I must rely on common sense. It's conceivable that Nicolae Ceaucescu, distrustful by nature and fearful of an "international conspiracy" against him ever since the accelerated development of the situation in Eastern block countries, took measures to organize a resistance in the event of an uprising. A secret order from the Interior Minister (no. 2600-1988) established a certain number of provisions in the event of such a situation: shock and intervention troops with the mission to resist until order was established, an arsenal of weapons to use if the need should arise, specially equipped apartments able to serve as logistical bases for commando operations and so on. Naturally, if a resistance was effectively begun from one of these locations, the professionals who knew about them and who had access to them also knew not to leave any traces.

I rule out, on the other hand, the participation of notorious "Arab terrorists" of whom there has been much imaginative speculation. It is easy to imagine the damage that would have been caused by urban guerilla specialists called into action by a foreign power. It is also well established that Libya, which was mentioned quite a bit at the time, had withdrawn its nationals (students for the most part) at the beginning of the conflict.

I myself do not exclude the completely opposite hypothesis, namely, that there was never any organized resistance at all, that the special units which I have just mentioned, largely followed the general movement rallying for a new power structure. In this case, they would consist of a few scattered, simulated operations and a series of isolated acts by a few fanatics sincerely devoted to the dictator's quasi-religious cult of personality, very likely driven to desperation by having to answer for their actions. To these people we can add those who found it impossible to believe that such a regime could be overthrown and who feared retaliation once the uprising died down, perhaps also hoping to be compensated for their loyalty. In the general confusion, all kinds of people were armed in the first hours. At a moment when everyone suspected everyone else – and when the most impassioned revolutionaries seemed to see members of the Securitatea all around them, some expecting to be lynched for belonging to the system of repression, others convinced that these people would not let themselves go down without a fight – it is not unreasonable to believe that these isolated acts and blunders were transformed into actual gun battles and that an accumulation of incidents of this kind (whose true importance was impossible for us to determine) could have seemed to us like the start of a civil war. The accumulation of hatred was so great that we feared it. It was imperative to avoid it.

The first shots were followed by more shots, this time coming from neighboring buildings occupied by the services of the Central Committee. Our impromptu defenders retaliated immediately and the army hastened to follow on their heels by deploying inappropriate methods for the situation – canon fire to attack snipers who had long since left their spots for another one.

The fact that the first exchange of gunfire did not take place until six hours after Ceaucescu's escape makes one think that, at the beginning, his supporters' disarray was such that no one thought to act, and that it wasn't until the moment of some possibly accidental gunshots signaling a counter-attack that several of the fallen dictator's faithful servants came on the scene, and telling themselves that all was not lost, tried to regain power.

At that moment, we were not sure that we had won. We did not know where Ceaucescu was nor what means he had to defend his power. It was also impossible for us to know if this delayed reaction was unplanned or if it was the beginning of a real armed resistance. It was crucial to propose a plan to the people in order to rally the political forces into a new power structure.

Since it no longer seemed safe to us, we left the ex-Central Committee building by a back door. Under the threat of continuous fire, creeping along the walls with, among others, Gelu Voican Voiculescu whom I had just met, we came out onto Magheru Boulevard where, miraculously, and as a perfect sign of the surrealism of the situation, we found a taxi. We told the driver who we were and we asked him to drive us to the Defense Ministry. The military authorities, whom I could not reach by phone (especially General Stanculescu), had let me know that the Revolution could count on them – not surprising since I knew about the officers' and the troops' position, their resentment towards the fallen dictator, and their aspirations, those of an entire nation's for democracy.

A New Power is Set in Place

At the Defense Ministry, we attempted to take stock of the situation in the capital and in the rest of the country.

The people didn't feel the resentment towards the army that it felt towards the Securitatea and the police. Less compromised, the army represented a safe political element in that its commanders were neither capable of being accepted by the masses, if by chance such an idea entered their heads, nor were they capable of making their troops obey, if they had wanted to take over by force. At that time the army controlled the only reliable communication system within our borders, and was more or less a structure which we could rely on to maintain the vital functions of the State. We quickly put together a senior staff and established our general headquarters there, since that was the only place still functioning.

Then we established a liason with people at the Television station and in the ex-Central Committee building and agreed to meet at evening's end at the television headquarters to draft a ten-point program, the political plan of the Revolution.

Broadcast live by the radio and television, the "Communiqué to the country of the Council of the National Salvation Front" announced the fall of the old regime and the foundation of a new power. "We are living a historic moment. Ceaucescu's people, who led the country to disaster, have been chased from power. [...] This victory for the entire country is due to the spirit of sacrifice of people of all ethnicities, especially our admirable young people. [...] During this crucial moment, we decided to create the Council of the National Salvation Front, which relies on the army and groups together all of the country's judicious forces, of all ethnicities. [...] As of now, all of the power structures of Ceaucescu's clan have been dissolved. The government, the Council of the State and all of its institutions no longer exist. All of the power is now based in the Council of the National Salvation Front." The address also recommended setting up the CNSF in the departments, municipalities and communes and asked them to take the necessary measures for the development of economic and social life.

Then, the National Salvation Front proposed a ten-point program:

1. An end to one-party rule and the establishment of a pluralistic system of government.

2. Free elections.

3. Separation of the powers of the State. The creation of a new Constitution.

4. An end to administrative and bureaucratic methods and

a restructuring of the national economy in favor of free enterprise.

5. The restructuring of agriculture in favor of the small farmer. The immediate end to the destruction of villages.

6. The reorganization of the educational system. The elimination of ideological dogmas. New basis for the development of national culture, press, radio and television.

7. Respect of the rights and liberties of ethnic minorities.

8. The reorganization of commerce with the priority of satisfying the daily needs of the population.

9. A foreign good-neighbor policy of friendship and peace in the spirit of European integration.

10. A domestic and foreign policy serving the needs and interests of the development of the human being with absolute respect for the rights and liberties of man, including the right to free travel.

This program unequivocally reproduces the sense of our Revolution. It is the absolute negation of totalitarian communism and is in favor of the modern democracy which everyone fighting in the Revolution wanted.

These ten points express ideas which have certainly guided my political work for a long time, but I am not presumptuous enough to take credit for them. I am convinced that at that moment, all of those committed to changing Romanian society would have drafted a similar plan and they would have then acted as I did. I satisfied myself with noting the similarity of my lifelong convictions with the desires of a society determined to change the very essence of its economic, political and social structures. All the work that I have since undertaken works toward a political structure desired by all

Romanians and also corresponds to what I personally consider useful and beneficial for our society. Certain points of the declaration were achieved in the first few days, some later on, and a few are still unachieved. Everything has been done to accomplish these objectives, even if it is evident that there is a specific reason for each of these ten points which demands a particular rhythm, adapted to the realities under which we must operate. This I say implementation of a single process for which staggering is advisable over a long enough period of time.

The Revolution, thus, had a clear and precise set of objectives which underscores the urgency of the changes to undertake and suggests a certain hierarchy of priorities. The first was the establishment of a new power structure. We came up with a list of people likely to constitute the center. They were people known for having challenged the dictatorship or unknowns who were noticed because of their participation of the events in progress, having shown courage, enthusiasm and a sense of the collective interest. This was the first outline of the Council of the National Salvation Front (named after the idea of a university student who had sent a letter to Radio Free Europe a few months earlier claiming to be a member of a "front" destined to save the country from the disastrous state that the Ceaucescu dictatorship had plunged it into). This term had the advantage of summing up what we wanted to do while at the same time avoiding all political qualifications and enabling a collaboration of all forces in the common effort to rebuild Romanian society.

This list was completely improvised. It contained, first of all, people who were present: Petre Roman who was someone probably only known by myself since I had worked with his father, the director of Political Publications, and with him, as he was a hydro-energy specialist like me at the same time that I was President of the National Water Council; Dumitru Mazilu, well known thanks to Radio Free Europe and dismissed from his duties because of his opinions in favor of human rights – we were counting on his legal expertise to coordinate the creation of the new electoral law; Gelu Voican Voiculescu, a geologist, who like Petre Roman, had just appeared on the scene along with Ion Caramitru and Sergiu Nicolaescu, the former a famous actor, the latter a renowned filmmaker but who had both taken on a political role only at the moment of our first appearance on television. We also added the names of some notorious dissidents to the list including, Mircea Dinescu, Dorina Cornea, Laslo Tokes and Ana Blandiana. Then, the names of several ex-communist leaders who had dared to address a letter a few months earlier to Radio Free Europe denouncing the Ceaucescu dictatorship: Silviu Brucan, Alexandru Bârladeanu and Corneliu Manescu among others. Kirali Karol, ex-militant of the Executive Political Committee of the Covasna region where a large population of Sicules live represented the ethnic minorities. Then the military figures: Generals Stanculescu, Gusa and Voinea. We wanted this team to cut across all social categories, all political orientations and all ages so that the country could thus acknowledge them. Everyone proposed names of often unknown people who through their attributes and the manner in which they had stood the test of the past few years, were able to reinforce the representativeness and effectiveness of what the leadership of the new power structure should be. It was in this way that we came up with a list of thirty-five people, the first members of the CNSF.

We also immediately spoke to the nation through radio and television in order to let the people know about the envisioned reform program and to announce the formation of the Council, not forgetting to point out that it was "a provisionary structure established in an operational manner" and that "the list was still open to the proposals of all social forces having fought against the dictatorship and having overthrown it." In the days which followed, the list was completed with the addition of a few new members, among them the Presidents of the departmental and Bucharest city CNSF.

The new power structure was beginning to come into existence: still provisional, it had a program and was already starting to build administrative structures likely to take charge of managing the transition.

A Confusing and Dangerous Situation

The situation continued to be very unsettled. We had no idea about Ceaucescu's whereabouts and the gunfire continued, kept up, it was rumoured, by urban guerilla units whom no one knew about and whose importance what difficult for us to evaluate.

The most disturbing news – and which is still impossible to verify – was heard all around: a convoy of helicopters was headed towards Bucharest. Others had been spotted over the Danube Delta, or in Banat or elsewhere. A press agency announced that helicopters were crossing

Yugoslavia in the direction of the Romanian border. We were also told that battleships had appeared on the Black Sea, that very bloody confrontations were taking place in several towns and that acts of sabotage had damaged strategic facilities. Television, which had played a very important role in the general mobilization to support the Revolution, was also the source of dangerous misinformation. Well-meaning people sometimes in a state of extreme excitement hallucinated, giving the most far-fetched information to journalists who, in this critical state did not have the means to verify it and communicated it to the country and thus contributed to the state of disorganization and panic.

General Gusa himself, the Senior Staff Chief and who after the abolition of the Defense Ministry was put in charge of the armed forces, seemed unable to cope with the events. He nearly pushed us off a very dangerous cliff by demanding that the people evacuate the streets so that the troops could more easily move around. It was a huge mistake in that it could have flared up the masses, already wary of a military strike to take power and also because in any case the crowd in the streets was not only the sign of our legitimacy, but also our principal support in case of a civil war, a possibility we still had not dismissed.

We asked General Militaru on December 24 to take charge of the Defense Ministry which had not had a leader since December 22, when General Milea supposedly committed suicide. Despite the fact that the chain of command was not functioning at all or very badly at best, General Militaru kept his calm and was in control of the situtation in the days that followed, but without enough power to avoid serious incidents due to the confusing situation which reigned throughout the country.

Many people died during these days due to the problems in controlling a spontaneous movement, the anarachic circulation of information and the multitude of initiatives which, since no one knew about them, no one could coordinate. The power unexpectedly given to us did not offer us effective tools to control the situation and to appease the crowd, to reassure everyone and to end the suspicions which were becoming muderous. Thus, when news spread of an imminent attack on the Otopeni airport, a number of students from the Câmpina Military Academy were sent to help another group to defend it. But because of a lack of communication, neither group knew about the other. In addition, while the Câmpina soldiers were on their way to Otopeni and no longer in contact with the Defense Ministry, they were warned by well-meaning people that the airport was already occupied by Ceaucescu supporters. This confusing and uncontrollable situation was the source of a tragedy: 48 dead and 17 wounded. The two groups who were supposed to defend a strategic point began to shoot at each other, those at the airport believing they were under attack and the others determined to dislodge those whom they believed to be the enemy.

A similar incident happened in front of the Defense Ministry, which was coming under fire from surrounding buildings. The soldiers and the officers in charge of defending it were neither trained nor prepared to respond to this kind of attack. General Militaru ordered a special anti-terrorist unit belonging to the Securitatea to the scene to fend off the attacks and also, it's said, to test their loyalties. The reinforcements arrived in several military vehicles. But those who were defending the building, not having been told and seeing the vehicles charge toward the entrance, opened fired.

Concerning these two massacres, it is suspected that the press assiduously exploited the situation and that our adversaries repeatedly played them up – all the more so since the authorities in charge of investigating and coming to a verdict on this matter were not in a position to give precise and satisfactory answers until today.

Unfortunately, these were not the only tragic episodes of a confusing situation in which everybody distrusted one another. This hampered coordination and communication among those participating in this extraordinary Historic moment which shed the blood of so many innocent people. I express our gratitude to all those who sacrificed their lives to give us the liberty and the dignity which we enjoy today.

There was a lot of fantasy about a "brotherly" aid that I had supposedly requested from the Soviets. Without even bothering to check facts, whose absurdity would have been easy to verify, certain people claimed that on the afternoon of December 22, I went to the Soviet Embassy to contact Moscow – that there, accompanied by Mr. Brucan, I even gave a press conference on Bulgarian television! That day I was not alone for a single moment. A crowd of witnesses have established precisely where I was at each moment, cutting short these attacks from people who already wanted to discredit me and in turn discredit the new power.

We have to clarify that during these days and nights, the only telephone contact with Moscow was established by the commanding group of the army senior staff and especially by General Gusa, who brought up the possiblity of Soviet logistical or technical support which we all judged inappropriate. In any case, I can confirm that the Council of the National Salvation Front never considered asking for help and that everyone found such an idea unacceptable. When asked about this, Mikhail Gorbachev himself made it clear that such a request was never solicited by the new Romanian power and that the Soviets had already decided not to intervene in any way in the unfolding events in its former satellite countries[1].

In situations where we neither have reliable information at our disposal nor time to make allowances, our mind func-

---

1. By chance, I came into the possession of a text which was part of a book written by two American political analysts, Michael Beschloss and Stube Talbott, titled "At the Highest Levels." This text contains very interesting passages concerning the events in Romania. For example: "On Sunday December 24, James Baker, the US Secretary of State, said during a program broadcast on NBC that 'the United States would not have any objection if the Warsaw Pact forces considered it necessary to intervene in Romania.'" The authors found the situation unbelievable: ten years after the Soviet invasion of Afghanistan by Brezhnev, and only a few weeks after Gorbachev took a stand against the Brezhnev Doctrine, an American Secretary of State was suggesting that the United States could favorably see a Soviet decision to send troops into an Eastern European country.

We can assume that James Baker had something else in mind when expressing his wish to see an end to the bloodbath. The United States had just launched Operation "Just Cause," a massive invasion of Panama whose principal goal aside from removing General Manuel Noriega from power was kidnapping him so he could be judged before the Miami courts for drug trafficking. A deployment of troops by Gorbachev would have been a counterpoint to action led by the United States in the Phillipines and in Panama. This would have tacitly established a new Soviet-American entente giving the two superpowers the implicit "right" to offer military aid to support "just causes" in their respective spheres of influence.

James Baker cabled his Moscow ambassador, Mr. Matlock, to sound out Soviet attitudes and intentions towards Romania. Mr. Matlock's inquiry at the Central Committee and the Foreign Ministry provoked the stupefication of certain Soviet officials, who wondered if the Americans weren't trying to trap them or engage them in a kind of provocation. The Soviets suspected Bush and Baker of wanting to make the Soviet Union return to its past behavior, which had proven very harmful for the USSR. Clearly, if Soviet forces had poured into Romania, the United States would not have missed this opportunity to publicly condemn the intervention,

tions as if in a strange acrobatic act. These few days and nights when everything was decided, I let myself get carried away by a kind of diffused wisdom accumulated throughout my lifetime called intuition. I mean that whatever my analysis of the political acts accomplished during these dangerous hours may be, we can rejoice in having made, in this urgent state, the choices which have spared the country of chaos and anarchy.

The Trial of Nicolae Ceaucescu

The fate of Nicolae Ceaucescu and his wife was played out in exceptional circumstances, in a violent confrontation which we feared might ignite a civil war.

With the passing of the hours, more victims would be added to all the others who had fallen during the days preceding the dictatorship's fall. The gunfire was intensifying and we couldn't estimate the strength of the side defending the overthrown regime. All that, when added to the panic and suspicion which reigned throughout the entire country, had provoked an emotional climate from which we could fear the worst. If the crowd had placed their hands on Nicolae Ceacescu and his wife, they would have lynched them without the slightest hesitation, without anyone wanting to or daring to defend them.

It was under these circumstances that we learned, on the morning of December 23, that Nicolae Ceaucescu had

---

thus taking the clear advantage with respect to global political opinion. Shevardnadze chose a less conspiratorial position; he informed Matlock that he believed Baker's suggestion to be, if not sinister, then at the very least "stupid" and he said he was "categorically" opposed to any foreign intervention in Romania. "The Romanian Revolution is their problem. Any Soviet intervention would transform Ceaucescu into a martyr."

This is the information and commentary presented by these two American analysts. I will abstain from any commentary.

been arrested and was being detained in a small military outpost near Târgoviste.

Concerned with bringing the fighting to an end, we first of all had to remove all hope to all units and fanatics capable of continuing to fight as long as the fallen dictator was still alive; we were scared that they believed that once he returned to power, he would be merciless with those who had not defended him to the very end. Likewise we were conscious that the military unit responsible for special prisoners did not have the means to resist a possible attack by his followers – what we feared all the more since army radars had recorded signals which led us to believe that helicopters were roaming the area.

The members of the brand new Bureau for the Council of the National Salvation Front who had been able to meet in these difficult conditions decided to immediately organize the trial of the fallen dictator. Indeed, to postpone it to when justice could be peacefully exercised, in a country just having returned to a Constitutional State, would have brought us considerable political capital. But did we have the right and the time to wait? For us, moved to recognize that Nicolae Ceacescu's stubborn hold on power made him responsible for the continuing bloodshed, there was no doubt as to the trial's outcome, and the decision was clear in our own minds. Even if, at first, I didn't share the opinion of those who were demanding an immediate trial, I considered, once the decision was taken, that it should be carried through and I accepted it by letting go of my doubts of conscience.

We then debated how to best organize the trial and the best time for it.

Our decision was determined by two simple reasons, whose obviousness left no room for doubt. First reason: we believed that Nicolae Ceaucescu's death would end all resistance since if support remained for him from social and political forces still willing to defend him, they would end all fighting upon learning of his death. Second reason: the detention center was not very secure and the confusion which reigned throughout the country did not allow us to take the risk of transferring him, which would have given this desperate man a chance to escape and to mobilize forces still loyal to him, and whose strength we were unaware of. We also feared personal acts of vengeance.

We had General Stanculescu organize the trial right there, in the same military base where Ceaucescu was being secretly detained. At our request, he contacted the Justice Ministry and the Supreme Court so this trial could take place in the best conditions under the circumstances, and that it respect the regulations in force as much as possible. The Council also sent Gelu Voican Voiculescu and Virgil Magureanu to be present at the trial. I will only say that the emotional climate which troubled us all also affected this improvised court of justice, whose every member knew of his responsibility before history, taken on before a country where blood was still flowing.

From my point of view, it was an act of popular justice accomplished under unique psychological conditions, even if personally, I couldn't share in the jubilance that the population let burst in the streets upon learning of his execution. Everything in my education, culture and convictions finds it unacceptable to execute another human being. The shock I felt when I had to bend to necessity – a feeling shared by others as well – was perhaps one of the reasons for which one of the first acts of the new power was to abolish the death penalty.

The videotape of the trial and execution of the dictatorial couple was taken to the Defense Ministry by General Stanculescu. We made one copy but expurgated certain scenes. In fact, it seemed preferable to us for their security not to show the faces of those who had been the "judges." The particularly gruesome images of the execution and the bodies were also eliminated since they had nothing to do with the political message we wanted to send.

We sent this version to the television station, setting off incredibly intense reactions. The journalist Victor Ionescu threatened to shoot Sergiu Nicolaescu (who had delivered the tape), if we didn't immediately hand over the original. Our explanations were finally sufficiently convincing that Ionescu agreed to air the tape as is. Afterwards, however, the pressure was so great and the rumor that the execution had not taken place circulated so persistently we saw ourselves forced to hand over a second tape ending with the horrible, unbearable images of the execution, which provoked an understandable emotional reaction, especially abroad.

The Ghost of the Securitatea

Privileged instrument of the repression during the years of the communist regime, having exerted a terror for these last twenty years which was above all psychological but none the less violent, the Securitatea is responsible for very serious social trauma. Still today, like a cinder which feels like it is still in our eye long after having removed it, many people believe that the Securitatea is still among us, ready to be reborn from its ashes, continuing to manipulate the power from the shadows.

Placed under the army control from the first hours of the Revolution, it immediately lost the rights and tools which made it such a dreaded and unique institution: its total decision-making autonomy, the right to arrest and investigate without any judicial control, its own detention facilities, and an independent armed force. The forces of the Securitatea did not put up any resistance – it is one of the reasons why what could have turned into a murderous civil war ended up limiting itself to acts of individual resistance. It is also true that to respond to these individual acts, we no longer had an adequate tool. We had to call in the army, whose heavy weaponry caused considerable damage that would have been avoided had we been able to turn to the special units of the Securitatea. Unfortunately, in the given circumstances this would have been inconceivable. Firstly, because we were not sure of their loyalty towards the new power and, secondly, because the people saw it as the most detestable expression of the former regime. Upon its abolition, we sorely lacked the tool needed to confront the violent political forces which were putting our fragile democracy in danger.

Once the Securitatea was abolished as an institution, we took the necessary steps to purge the army of its undesirable elements who had belonged to the system of repression. The military authorities took charge of this purge, whose importance goes far beyond everything that was done in the other institutions inherited from the former regime or in other countries. The officers responsible for the repression, especially at the moment of the Revolution, and those who had had political responsibilities were given justice.

A great number of Securitatea staff, whom we could not charge with anything, nevertheless preferred to leave the army by resigning or by asking to be pensioned off. For those who we could not conclude as having had political positions or responsibilies in the activities of the repression, we re-assigned a part of them within the various army services. Another group, consisting of intelligence specialists, was used for the Romanian Intelligence Service, a body created in April 1990, whose role and functions exclude all repressive action, and which is subject to all the norms governing this kind of activity in any democratic country. The officers coming from the old Securitatea represent a very low percentage of those working in this new organization.

During January 1990, in the presence of the media, specialists from the army and the Telecommunications and Postal Service Ministry dismantled and rendered inoperational the center for the Securitatea's listening devices, as well as all of the facilities formerly used to spy on the people. This was not enough to dissipate the people's mistrust of the Romanian intelligence service, which for some people was the heir of the Securitatea and whose duties and abuses they feared it would perpetuate. Accused without proof of illegal phone taps, the service was several times forced to investigate and turn up irrefutable material proof of hoaxes to clear itself of having installed bugs in editorial offices or private apartments. Any person proven guilty of abuses reminiscent of the Securitatea's practices is immediately dismissed. Knowing that it is the Securitatea's heir, but forced by the nature of its duties to not be as open as all the other State institutions, the Romanian Intelligence Service has continually reported its most minor acts and deeds to the political authorities. Moreover, in accordance with the law that governs its operation, a specially appointed parliamentary commission closely watches over all its activities.

Concerning the opportunity to publish the list of Securitatea informers and to give all citizens the chance to consult their files, Parliament, after lengthy debate, finally found it wiser to make these files public only after 40 years. A special commission of Parliament can nevertheless study and propose the publication of certain files which may be currently of particular interest.

Numerous manuscripts are also found in the files inherited from the Securitatea. Some members of the Romanian Intelligence Service, unfortunately few and not very trained in the matter, are trying to piece together the scattered sheets in order to identify and locate the authors, or those having legal right to these texts, to allow them to recover these manuscripts, which belong to our intellectual heritage of the last forty years. This is how Humanitas Publishers printed a collection of unpublished texts by the philosopher Constantin Noica and how the daughter of poet Ion Caraion, who died in Switzerland, was informed she could end up with her father's manuscripts. This was also the case with the writer Petre Dumitriu.

Indeed, after all that we have lived through, the suspicion of public opinion should not surprise us. Nevertheless, placed under the control of the legislative branch and the

High Defense Council, the new Romanian Intelligence Service functions today on legal grounds, conforming to the customary jurisdiction of a Constitutional State.

A Democracy is Established

Recovering our History

The destiny of every revolution plays itself out the day after victory. The night before, when tensions were rising without any hope of a political outcome, Romanians had only one idea in their heads: overthrow the dictatorship that was crushing them – at whatever price necessary, without thinking much about what would happen next.

When the structures of the old regime collapsed one after the other, nothing had been set up to replace them. Thus, Romanian society found itself in a chaotic atmosphere and in danger of anarchy. The social boiling point had been reached and people were no longer in a position to control anything. We were confronted with a wave of demands. All of the social groups wanted justice at the same time right away. In the beginning of 1990, we were often on the verge of catastrophy. We were in the middle of a institutional and legislative void, paralyzed by a serious authority crisis. In administration, the educational system, the economy and transportation no one recognized anyone else's authority any more. People were wandering about in total confusion. The old institutions had been abolished and the new ones had not yet been established. The new power structures, decided by democratic bills, had barely been sketched out on the legislative plan and could not, before the May 20, 1990 vote, rely on the support of the legitimate authority of a general election.

The absence of authority allowed for the rapid flare-up of conflicts, sometimes even violent and indomitable, several times coming close to civil or ethnic war. The disintegration of Eastern European societies had just begun and no one was able to foresee the cruelty of the confrontations which would soon to leave this part of the world tragically bloodstained.

Nicolae Ceaucescu's regime not only compromised its own period in history, but also the future by having no concern for it. Refusing all forms of domestic opposition, the regime had not allowed for the appearance of elements likely to prepare for this huge change. When the change finally happened, we were caught off guard. We had no new generation of political leaders capable of assuming the enormous task of totally modifying the structures of an entire country. At the moment of the collapse of the old regime, Romanian society was, thus, unprepared for an upheaval of this magnitude.

We did not have a coherent and global plan to carry out the transition towards a market economy and a democratic society. The Revolution was a "jump into the void" for us. It was the expression of the height of despair and not that of a vision of the future. This explains the untold difficulties that we encountered on the road to transition.

Hungary or Poland, for example, prepared for two or three decades for the turning points which came about in 1989. In these countries, when the replacement of the old regime – almost naturally dying out – became possible, quite a few economic reforms had already been accomplished and the national perspectives were fairly clearly defined. This was not the case with Romania; at the time we were able to begin reforms, a political revolution had already consumed a large part of the country's energies. Our neighbors were pursuing their reforms in a new political context, but we had to start from scratch.

This way of looking at things explains a certain number of troubling phenomena. After the December 1989 Revolution, a group of notable intellectuals and journalists – probably out to clear their names of past submission, indeed of their complicity with the fallen regime – believed it their duty to contest the newly elected power in an absolute and obstinate manner. To the point that they actually believed that what they had not otherwise accomplished could be made up for by the systematic harassment of those whom the country had freely entrusted with political responsibilities. This form of opposition, whose only goal is destruction, led by people who were afraid to say YES because they had not known how to say NO when it was necessary, put on a negative production after the Revolution. Instead of tackling their own biographies and a History from which they had more or less experienced the painful tests and, incapable of resolving their own problems of conscience, these last-minute opponents exercised their wits to invent and fabricate enemies in order to cheaply buy themselves a dubious political glory.

Imagine a phenomenon where the causes and effects are simultaneous. This was the case for us; a Revolution surprised by its own radicalism, lacking the conditions and forces needed to transform it into reality; a Revolution forced to invent and build its foundations after the fact, trying hard to quickly put everything which should have preceded it into place.

Revolutions are extreme solutions, applicable to heightened crisis situations where there is no other way out. It certainly would have been preferable that the passage from one political system to another be done in stages, like in other Eastern and Central European countries which did not have to pay the enormous social and human price of such a convulsion. It is true that Revolutions also have a therapeutic effect; they force you to leap ahead, but for a long time exhaust the societies that are recovering from such a shock. Paradoxically, revolutions often impede the natural evolution of a society. Periods of progress in leaps and bounds are followed by periods of stagnation, alternations which interrupt the continuous accumulation of history and harmonious development. The countries which have replaced their communist systems with relative ease are more stable today and farther along the path of reform. On the other hand, we had to immediately undertake reforms which other countries were able to establish over time. Once again, Romania has constrained itself from advancing by changing in its course. How can we develop when every fifty years we destroy everything and head in a new direction? There are always considerable historic costs to a revolution, and Romania is still paying the price for its December 1989 uprising.

The First Convulsions

The first half of 1990 was a period of incessant political upheaval for Romania. Starting in January, several dozen political parties were established with the hope of giving the country a parliamentary life modeled after

Western democracies. Often, because of a doctrine, a team or a leader, these parties were content either to bring back pre-World War II models or to translate foreign slogans into Romanian. They seemed more concerned with finding a stepping stone to power than searching out an electoral base. They did not try to understand the people on whose behalf they were speaking or the fact that they were the population's choices, people whom they were asking for the right to lead Romanian society.

It is, perhaps, premature to note that the political heritage of forty years of communism is not located where certain people would like to see it, namely in the positions of responsibility of some of the four million card-carrying members of the Party, but rather in an unfortunate tendency to scorn that which is the foundation of all democracy, that is, the outcome of the polls and the will of the voters. A new supposedly intellectual "avant garde" considers the popular electorate too inept at making political choices to be entrusted with a ballot and incapable of knowing where their real interests lie, which this "elite" claims to be more qualified to define and defend. This opinion has the right to exist just as any other one does, as long as those who share it are honest enough not to call this plan for the restoration of the minority dictatorship "democratic." This was also the opinion of a certain publication, shocked that on the outcome of various elections, the everyday Romanian did not make the "right choice." Apparently, an editorial staff or a correspondent was sent to the scene for a couple of hours and seduced by a handful of intelligent men, cultured, perhaps, but for whom the people are only an intellectual projection, a much too abstract construction to allow them to take into account the every day concerns of life. From a political point of view, this elitist and idyllic fashion of seeing things hides, in fact, much contempt, an attitude which has always worked well with authoritarianism but also with dilettantisme, the spirit of vague desire and a radicalism dangerous to the social fabric. In fact, the temptation of political monopoly is always present, even if now it has another origin.

I think that a true democracy calls for the strong conviction that the majority of people have an implicit awareness of the collective good. The minority accepts the will of the majority with good will, convinced that it is the best solution for everyone, including those having another point of view. If not, the country's strengths are wasted in meaningless confrontations, the political world becoming the terrain of incessant guerilla warfare and democracy a continual sports competition; we forget where we started and our goals for the future – a prosperous life and a chance for everyone to fulfill their dreams.

At the same time that the embryonic political parties were being established in the first days of 1990, I also saw political powers appear which refused the democratic functioning of the State. Groups of all kinds, too much a minority to have even the slightest chance (at least in the immediate future) of gaining power, or seduced by the enthusiasm of a crowd of demonstrators led by improvised politicians refusing to admit that they represented a fringe element of the population. In other cases, foreign pressure kept up an agitation with no regard for national interests. Benefitting from new found liberty, these groups tried to impose by force political solutions which were slightly or completely acceptable. At the same time that the new government was endeavoring to install democratic rule and was preparing for free elections (which finally took place after five months), and at the same time that the fledgling opposition was finding the institutional framework which would permit it to participate in politics, the entire process was threatened by attempts to seize power by totally undemocratic means.

The first strike took place on January 12, scarcely three weeks after the abolition of the dictatorship.

It was at the moment when, in orthodox tradition, a religious service was supposed to take place for the victims of the Revolution. There was a ceremony planned in Timisoara and I made the mistake of asking Mr. Dumitru Mazilu, vice-president of the Council for the National Salvation Front, to represent me. Sorely resented, this move on my part was seen as me brushing aside those who had been the foundations of the Romanian Revolution. I feel that I provoked, through this blunder, a reaction of distrust which had no good reason and which was very harmful in this troubled period when the most important thing was for well-meaning people to unite their efforts and consolidate our new democracy. But in Bucharest, the tension was great. Fearing serious consequences, it seemed dangerous for me to stay away.

I was not mistaken.

Processions, wreath laying and religious services took place throughout the day, and, as is the custom, people were spilling drops of wine on the tombs to honor the victims and to show them our gratitude. In the evening, a crowd gathered at Victory Square in front of Government

Headquarters. The demonstrators were so excited that it was clear that they had not been pushed by an urgent desire for sensible demands. Some people found the occasion ripe to politically exploit this excitement, hoping to strike a blow against the still fragile power, which was now leading the country because of the popular movement whose energy these individuals wanted to imitate.

We had to beware of this. During the turmoil of a revolution, the people in the streets can defend very different causes with equal amounts of passion and one form of popular expression can convey, just a few days or hours later, radically different political opinions. When free elections still had not taken place – the conditions were still not right – only political analysis enabled us to distinguish the underlying trends of opinion from superficial demands which only expressed the interests of an agitated minority. The latter was taking place; the demands of the January 12 rally called into question two of the fundamental democratic measures decreed by the Council for the National Salvation Front, namely the abolition of capital punishment and freedom of opinion.

I remember that one of the new government's first measures – which wanted to thus show what political philosophy it subscribed to – had been the abolition of capital punishment. After instituting freedom of speech and assembly, it had seemed wrong for the new government to inaugurate the measures by outlawing the Communist Party – which had anyway self-destructed, no one attempting to take on such a weighty heritage. Its principal leaders had been arrested and were going to be judged in accordance with their alleged penal guilt, but not in any way for their political opinions. No one had had the idea to register it on either of the two lists of parties being organized. Its property, which was mixed up with the State's, was naturally transferred over to the new Government.

A Power Unable to Defend Itself

The crowd swarming in front of Government Headquarters on January 12, 1990 was making two demands: the reintroduction of capital punishment and the outlawing of the Communist Party.

We began by trying to establish discussion with them. Unfortunately, just having returned from Timisoara, Dumitru Mazilu, vice president of the National Salvation Front, went to speak to the protesters and only excited them more. Those following him – Ion Caramitru, Gelu Voican Voiculescu and Petre Roman – could not make themselves be heard either. Against the opinion of those surrounding me, I decided to go there myself. It's true that anything could have happened; I had previously felt this kind of electricity which emerges from a riled-up crowd surpassing physical laws and the logic of natural phenomena. But in any case, I did not think that they would turn against me.

After having succeeded in calming their spirits a bit, I invited a delegation to come and talk to some government representatives who were there. During the discussion, I understood two things: first of all, that it was not about political demands (they wanted to re-establish capital punishment to use it on such and such a person who would have threatened such and such an interest, or to outlaw the

Communist Party to eliminate a dangerous force, at that time already being pulled along in a hearse). It was in fact about symbolic demands. Symbols are troublesome since they are singular and whole; they are not negotiable and do not lend themselves to compromise. Second observation: these people, whose excitement was such that they seemed ready to do anything, had spent the entire day grieving for the dead. Their two demands were not even ideological in spirit but more nearly religious: like pouring wine on tombs, they needed, for the eternal rest of the dead, symbolic culprits (communists, Securitatea people) to metaphorically shed a drop of blood (the re-establishment of capital punishment) on the ground where the heroes of the Revolution lay. Did I have to take into account this kind of mindstate? I told myself that they were emotional demands which stood a good chance of not resurfacing the next day and which would not seriously call into question the progress of our democracy. How to react? And above all, what means did I have at my disposal to re-establish order and defend the still fragile and vulnerable State institutions?

This requires an explanation, all the more necessary since it defines under what conditions the government had to act during this period.

It is necessary to remember two obvious facts which seem to have escaped a good many of the commentators examining the realities of Eastern Europe. The first is related to the difficulty of reacting in a post-revolutionary period to street demonstrations of, apparently, the same nature as those that brought you to power. The second stems from the difficulty, during these conditions, of providing a police force accepted by everyone and not a tool of repression seen as an instrument to take away power, which would risk putting the social order in danger.

What was happenning was proving conclusively that in a few days and hours a street demonstration could express very different, indeed, contradictory ideas. It had the same force as the one which was first stirred up for the ideal of liberty and then it let itself be won over by chaos, or by different social groups which were using a form of popular expression valued by the Revolution for reprehensible ends. Clearly, if we wanted to save the country from needless turmoil, we had to avoid at all costs giving the impression, right or wrong, of gagging this kind of popular expression, thus bringing together into an inopportune solidarity all those who would have immediately reacted in the name of the newly recovered freedom of protest. The only wise solution to the crises which were going to shake the country in the first half of 1990 appeared to us to be discussion and compromise. On principle, we ruled out repression, the job of the police simply being a deterrent, with a formal ban on resorting to weapons, even in the case of an attack. We must absolutely take this into account in order to understand this period of transition – which is still not completely finished.

During almost this entire period, the government in charge of replacing the political structures of the dictatorship with those of a true democracy in a Constitutional State, found itself lacking the appropriate means to preserve public order and to defend the institutions.

On the evening of January 12, 1990, after weighing the pros and cons, the seriousness of the political danger, the weakness of my means of intervention against the crowd of demonstrators and the emotional circumstances which could lead to the worst, I decided to give in. We drew up a decree restoring capital punishment and outlawing the Romanian Communist Party. Denounced a day later, of course, by the Council for the National Salvation Front, without raising the slightest protest. This about-face that we had to make on the evening of January 12 allowed us to avoid a serious crisis and to preserve, at the price of a little dignity, our still fragile democratic achievements.

Was I wrong or was I right? Certain members of the Council for the National Salvation Front blamed me for this provisionary concession. But no one knows what could have happened if we had not given in at that moment. Perhaps nothing. But did we have the right to take the risk?

January 28

On January 28, everything was repeated in another context.

At that moment, some thirty political parties were in existence, among them the National Farmer's Party, the National Liberal Party, the Social Democratic Party and so on. I had already met their leaders several times to get acquainted with their political orientations. With the National Salvation Front having decided to abandon its image of the gatherer of all political components to become a party like the others, I wanted to create a Council which, in this period of transition, had to represent all Romanians – whose electoral choices no one knew yet – and which would link together all of these new political groups. Together, we laid the foundations of the Provisionary Council for National Unity, which allowed all the political groups of the moment to participate in the preparation of the first free elections.

On January 27, the leaders of the three principal parties cited above (combined, they would receive three months later just 12% of the votes) informed me that they were planning to organize two rallies the next day ending up in front of Government Headquarters. I advised against it; tension still reigned in the streets and uncontrollable rebels might take advantage of this to provoke disorder under the guise of a political demonstration, whose legitimacy would otherwise be inarguable. The party leaders pretended to understand my arguments. Although they had the means to contain outbursts thanks to their security staff, they said, they were abandoning the idea for this march. Moreover, we agreed to appear together on television to calm nerves and to inform the people that there was a dialogue between the power and this incipent opposition and that we were determined to work together to establish a parliamentary democracy. Unfortunately, I found myself in front of the cameras with only Petre Roman. The absence of the representatives of these three parties was all the more regretable since the militants of the National Salvation Front also had a meeting with their supporters; this could lead to confrontations which were better to avoid.

In spite of the promises, the opposition's demonstrators invaded Victory Square, where Government Headquarters are. Perhaps even surpassing the organizers' intentions (at least that's what they said afterward), overrunning a powerless security staff, a part of the crowd attacked the Government Headquarters.

I immediately invited the political leaders to a discussion on television. I attempted to understand their political plans and the goal of this violent demonstration. In all sincerity, given that we were in perfect agreement on the political goal to hold elections as soon as possible, it seemed to me that the only real demand was that the people who were provisionally exercising power give that place to others and they had no other argument for this power exchange than simply their desire for it. Imprisoned for 17 years for his political opinions, Corneliu Coposu, leader of the National Farmer's Party, had suffered tremendously and with the greatest dignity. Once again, as long as the ballot box had not returned its results, it was difficult to conceive of a political order while everyone was outdoing each other by brandishing their carte blanche privileges. I nevertheless promised myself to hasten the formation of the Provisionary Council for National Unity to allow all the political forces to participate in the decisions.

We were still seated around this round table when Government Headquarters were assaulted. I immediately proposed to Coposu, the principal organizer of this demonstration, to accompany me so that together we could attempt to calm them down. Forced by the facts to recognize that the reassuring remarks uttered the night before were baseless, Coposu responded that he had no authority over the demonstrators. In fact, when we finally left and he tried to address the crowd, no one listened to him. Once again, because of some people's carelessness, whose good faith I do not question but rather their political wisdom, we were confronted with a problem difficult to resolve within our means. The people in the street took charge of the problem, without our consent of course, and without taking into consideration what seemed desirable to us; upon learning that the demonstrators were trying to invade Government Headquarters, the members of the National Salvation Front, who considered themselves the champions of the political values of the Revolution, came running to defend a legitimate power which they perceived in jeopardy. A confrontation ended that day, luckily without any serious repercussions, only to be followed by much angrier blow-ups the next day.

It is necessary to note – and later election results left no doubt about it – that the National Salvation Front also had many supporters who sometimes were part of the same violent social strata of the population. Having judged the attitudes of the leaders of the opposition as ambiguous and disloyal during the discussion that we had with them on television at the time of the riot, and under the influence of the shocking images aired by the television station showing Government Headquarters being attacked by the crowd, our "supporters," over whom we had no control, went down into town, driven by a spirit of revenge. They sacked the headquarters of several parties and we had to intervene immediately and impose our authority in order to prevent matters from getting worse. It is necessary to understand that in a period of trouble, when institutions are changing completely and when the people in the street have not fully finished exercising the rights given to them in the Revolution, any political act perceived as violent or disloyal risks causing a response. Wisdom would have wanted all provocations to be avoided. But our political adversaries, whom we were hoping to meet in an electoral debate and not in the street, did not always share this opinion. We had not seen the end of our struggles!

In February, a crowd of protesters again invaded Government Headquarters and sacked it by threatening to kill the ministers inside. Once again, we tried to calm people's spirits without resorting to force, which possibly gave the idea to some people that power is easier to seize through violence than through elections.

The Provisional Council for National Unity

Toward the middle of January 1990, barely three weeks after the Revolution, I had already begun negotiations with the leaders of the recently established political groups in order to include them in the decisions taking place during that transition period and in the preparation of the elections scheduled to take place May 20 – just five months after the popular movement had sent Romania on the road to democracy. Despite the troubles which took place on January 12 and 28, these discussions allowed for the creation, on February 1, of the Provisional Council for National Unity.

The National Salvation Front, an umbrella organization representing the various political trends appearing at the time of the Revolution, held 90 seats, leaving the same

number to the new parties whom we could assume represented the seeds of opposition. Ethnic minority parties
who had just been formed had the right to supplementary
seats, added to the 180 original seats. This Council was already a prototype of parliament, in charge of drawing up
the decree-law that we needed to organize the first free
elections, based on agreed-upon constitutional principles:
the form of the State (at that moment, no one questioned
the idea of a republic, which appeared to all of us clear and
natural), the structure of Parliament, the institution of the
Presidency, the voting method for the election of the two
houses and the president, etc. These principles were in-
cluded in a separate chapter of the electoral bill drawn up
in January by a legal committee and representatives of different political parties, and then ratified by the Provisional
Council for National Unity.

Aired in their entirety on television into the late hours of
the night, the Committee meetings were followed with
great interest throughout the country, which was learning
the advantages and limitations of democracy.

The Provisional Council for National Unity worked like a
true parliament. After being examined at length by the
designated tri-party committee, and after debates which
went over its provisions point by point for six days, the
Provisional Council for National Unity adopted the electoral law and the measures concerning the organization of
the campaign. Certain radical opposition groups, like a few
anti-communist organizations, proposed that we legally
ban people who had occupied important functions before
December 1989 from running in the elections. This idea
which was coming back with a lot of persistence in the

media targeted me directly, as well as a few former leaders of the Communist Party, several of whom ended up openly contesting the dictatorship, such as Corneliu Manescu, a long-time Foreign Minister. In view of Romanian reality, such a provision would have been absurd. I recall that even later, in 1992, all six presidential candidates were former party members, and one of them had also been a member of the Soviet Communist Party. Moreover, this makes us wonder what fate we should plan for the other former Romanian Communist Party members, if we were to punish those who had resisted from the inside?

In fact, as it appeared from the debates held at the time, such a provision would have been in complete disagreement with the spirit of our Revolution, which guaranteed everyone the right to think and to express his opinions freely. My political adversaries were finding it more advantageous to eliminate me through an administrative provision than to face me in the electoral battle. I was surprised to observe that a few champions of democracy could not find a better way to use this recovered freedom than by denying it to others.

At that point, having a Party card meant no more than having a driver's license. The comparison is more eloquent than it seems; to drive a car we have to prove that we know the code forbidding running a red light and turning against a one-way street – except if you decide to take a risk. As a practical matter, any remotely competent individual who wanted to succeed in his professional life was a Party member. With 4 million members in a country of 20 million, the Romanian Communist Party had become the packaging into which all of Romanian society fit. If we can indeed implicate individual responsibility, and if we can call to account people having taken advantage of the Party structure to commit socially blameworthy acts, then it is neither reasonable nor correct to evoke a collective guilt, which, in addition, would have at its origin a crime of opinion. And then, how do you distinguish those who took the Party card to give their careers a chance to grow and those who, not having any skills, took it with the simple goal of succeeding? Some people would like to force the former Communist Party militants to do hard labor to pay for their crimes – in other words, to reopen the camps!

However, pressure from the masses caused a de facto purge to take place starting from the first days of the Revolution. A spontaneous movement relieved everyone of their duties in the State system if they had compromised themselves by having an obsequious attitude towards the regime or by participating in the corruption of the dictatorship. It's true that they also dismissed quite a few competent men, managers with a lot of experience who, sometimes by taking important personal risks, had tried to jam the dictatorship's machinery and to salvage what it had to offer. This revolutionary process aided quite a few demagogues, amateurs and irresolute people of very questionable abilities, who had no specific qualifications. This did not take long to cause problems in handling this extremely difficult transition period.

While keeping an eye on government activity, which entailed regularly explaining its actions in front of the plenum or in the committees, the Provisional Council for National Unity also discussed and adopted a certain number of very important decree-laws, including those concerning privatization of small and medium-size enterprises, liberalization of commerce and services, foreign investment and the organization of mixed enterprises.

The Târgu Mures Events

Of course I wanted everything to return to order quickly and safely, but we were in the middle of election preparations.

After all that had happened, I could not have any illusions. I, nevertheless, thought that the forthcoming elections could calm spirits and advance us on the road to normality. That was my hope and I was hanging on to it. Unfortunately, springtime for Romanian politics had turbulence in the air. From the center of the country, signs of worrisome conflicts were reaching us. Circumstances prevented me from giving them the importance they needed and also from piecing together a complete image from the fragmented and sometimes contradictory information which would have led me to discover the warning signs of the inter-ethnic conflict which would explode in Târgu Mures on March 19, claiming victims on both sides.

Fueled from inside as well as from outside the country, the tensions between Romanians and Hungarians in Transylvania – whose origin goes a long way back – ended in violent confrontations that we cannot understand outside of the exceptional context that the country was going through.

I was convinced, and still am, that the fall of the dictatorship finally offered the necessary conditions for a peaceful and prosperous cohabitation of Romanians and the country's minorties. Since the Romanian people had not been any more favored by the old regime than these minorities, it appeared natural to me to preserve, under the new circumstances, the solidarity which had enabled us to resist the dictatorship and to then overthrow it. Unfortunately, this early consensus was quickly shattered by the clash of new divergent interests and already established groups – not only related to the country's political and economic transformations, but also to excessive and anachronistic nationalist agendas. In a climate of suspicion, mistrust and widespread confrontation, the old rivalries between communities were re-ignited, fueled by frustration and old resentments that the new political and economic reality were not able to appease.

The strongest personalities within the Hungarian community (Laszlo Tokes and Domokos Geza, for example), who would later lead the Democratic Union of Romanian Magyars (DURM), had their place within the country's authority structure ever since its establishment, and Karoly Kiraly was elected vice-president of the Provisional Council for National Unity. The proportional representation of minorities in this body strengthened our hopes of avoiding tensions and misunderstandings. One of the first documents of the new power, made public just a few days after the fall of the dictatorship, explicitly affirmed our intention to respect international norms and democratic principles concerning the rights of minorities to preserve, develop and express their ethnic, cultural, religious, and linguistic identity, not at all accepting the idea which some people were already talking about of giving special privileges to a specific group because of its ethnic origins.

Since the December 1989 Revolution, the new democratic institutions have made considerable efforts to guarantee (from legislative, political, administrative, and practical points of view) human and individual rights for all Romanian citizens of different ethnic origins and to assure the conditions necessary for them to preserve their identity, their cultural specificity, their language and their traditions.

Nevertheless, little by little, the DURM leadership (the principal political party of the Hungarian minority) started to adopt a rigid, intransigent and incomprehensible position. They were persistently asking with unsettling impatience and a particularly virulent tone for us to immediately meet demands which could only be solved in time, and after a sufficient psychological preparation, through laws and institutions which were still non-existent, at a time when we had just begun reconstructing the country's political and social structure from the ground up. Moreover, this was done in a climate where certain political groups (who were demanding power in virtue of supposed "historic rights" from fifty years before) found it profitable to attack us, using every little thing against us, and did not hesitate to exploit the national problem in a very dangerous way, leaving fearful ambiguities to hover over this question. The DURM's attitude was explained both by the radicalization of some of its leaders and by the pressure coming from various extremist circles of the Hungarian minority. Added to all of this were the echos of the electoral campaign taking place at that time in Hungary, where nationalist and irredentist positions had been stirred up with a certain persistence; some particularly disagreable comments concerning Romania and Romanians incited the Hungarian population to have an increasingly radical and unrealistic view of our country.

Certain outwardly hostile DURM leaders, especially Lazlo Tokes, accused the new power of pursuing the repressive policies of the old regime when it came to minorities. Such assertions, above all destined for foreign media use, made the Romanian people sound intolerant, xenophobic, chauvinistic and barbaric. These were unjust assumptions which deeply hurt the inhabitants of a country having proved throughout history to have exactly the opposite feelings.

I tried to convince the leaders of the DURM that the universal principles concerning human rights and those of a democratic society did not allow us to have two different sets of laws for the citizens of a country nor to implement different policies according to the national majority or minorities. I also tried to make them understand that the idea that the minorities' demands should be met immediately, as amends for the cruelty suffered during the dictatorship, while the same demands expressed by the national majority could wait, was discriminatory and perilous. The rhythm and the progress of the democratic process cannot be differentiated according to ethnic criteria, and the complex and dangerous problem of the relationships between communities could not be resolved overnight, especially when extremist explosions could threaten the general process of democratization and the still too new and fragile institutions.

In an open and unbiased dialogue, I tried to explain to them that their demands smacked of a dangerous separatism and were without a future. The legitimate worry of preserving a cultural identity never justifies the demand to politically and administratively institutionalize a territorial autonomy in flagrant contradiction with the country's historic, geographic and economic morphology and with its demographic realities (90% of the population is Romanian and there is no region where the Romanian population is not the majority; moreover, the densest clusters of Hungarian population are found in the center of the country, very far from the Hungarian border).

I also directed their attention to the fact that not a single international institution recognized the "collective rights" they were vehemently demanding, and that the concept of "community self-determination" which followed from it remained fuzzy and equivocal, leading to an absurd and unnatural separatism and the isolation of the Hungarian population in ghettos, a kind of "reserve" of a Magyar identity. This distressing situation benefitted no one, and was most harmful to those who wanted to defend it and forced people to live in close quarters and barely habitable buildings, poorly fed and cut off from their economic and cultural environment.

In order to understand the inflexible position of the Hungarian leaders, it is necessary to recall that at the time the media spoke of many plans for the federalization of Eastern Europe, some even wanting to rebuild, in a new configuration, the old Austro-Hungarian Empire, a necessary buffer zone, they said, needed to insure a balanced Europe. The dismantling of Eastern Europe with an implicit revision of borders even seemed like a tactic to integrate the populations of that region into the European

Community. And this idea is no doubt linked to the beginning of the Yugoslavian drama.

These scenarios which play upon diverse elements of political mythology and historical utopia would not have troubled the Romanian public so much if rumor had not attributed them to the famous Malta Conference which took place in 1989 where they were supposed to have decided to divide the world up in a new way. Repeated victims of such divisions in recent History, Romanians took this threat very seriously. The leaders of DURM ended up finding themselves in a head-on confrontation with the reality of the National Unified Romanian State, a reality that they began contesting the moment the new Constitution was adopted and which they continue to contest.

Thus, in January 1990, in the middle of the school year, the DURM leadership insisted that mixed schools be abolished where students were taking, in neighboring classrooms, classes in their respective native languages, and that they be replaced with "ethnically pure" establishments. With no prior negotiations and with very little preparation for such an important measure, without even attempting to obtain agreement from the parents and students, DURM organized street demonstrations and strikes pushing for the fulfillment of this demand, finally making the Minister of Education give in. I am sure that this provocation and this weakness on the State's part led to inter-ethnic conflicts which were already brewing in an increasingly explosive climate because of other diversions, aggravating suspicion and misunderstandings. The demands of certain organizations of citizens of Hungarian origin had become ultimatums ("Right here right now" and "Now or Never") and the upset intensifed, culminating in the Hungarian student strike at the Medical and Pharmaceutical Institute in Târga Mures from March 9 to 17.

The Romanian population was uneasy and, consequently, mobilized itself to confront the Hungarian population extremist movements. Thus, the cultural and civic organization "Valta Româneasca" was born, whose main concern is to defend the idea of unity and national identity in a territory where Romanians are the majority.

It is in this climate that certain leaders of the Hungarian community decided to celebrate, by a large demonstration scheduled to take place March 15, the date of the beginning of the Magyar Revolution of 1848 whose platform refused to recognize the national rights of Romanians and foresaw the "unification of Transylvania with Hungary" (this region was autonomous during the Austro-Hungarian Empire). At that time, rejoined by force to Hungary by revolutionaries, the majority Romanian population came around to the Austrian Emperor's side, fighting against Kossuth nationalists, whom the Romanians found guilty of horrible crimes and atrocities. To bring up, and even worse, to celebrate these events in 1990 was an irresponsible provocation. Some people took this risk.

Some 10,000 "tourists" coming from Hungary to reinforce the ranks of extremists already on the scene were the origin of several incidents in Satu Mare, Sovata and Târgu Mures and other places. They incited the population to violence, defied the Romanian authorities, scoffed at the Romanian flag and ensigns, displayed the Hungarian flag on public buildings, replaced Romanian signs with

Hungarian ones, sung the Hungarian national anthem in the streets and so on. This provoked a response from the Romanian population, who a few days later, organized counter-demonstrations and demanded sanctions against those who, by their attitude, had encouraged acts harmful to national dignity and which called the integrity of the State into question.

From then on, the demonstrations and counter-demonstrations came one after the other and reactions multiplied. On March 19, Romanians called for the dismissal of the departmental vice-president of the Provisionary Council for National Unity, Mr. Kincses Elod, accused of siding with those who were threatening the unity of the State. The demonstrators clashed with Hungarian counter-demonstrators. A violent confrontation followed, the public buildings were devastated and we were saddened by several casulaties, including the writer Suto Andras. The next day, the Hungarian population announced a general strike in support of Mr. Elod. Some 15,000 Hungarian demonstrators clashed with a third as many Romanians. Alerted by telephone, the inhabitants of surrounding villages showed up at Târgu Mures, provoking a chain of serious events. Passions exploded, and on the evening of March 20, the police were no longer able to intervene and contain the demonstrators who were armed with steel pipes, knives, hatchets, fire extinguishers and other makeshift weapons. The toll of these confrontations was particularly heavy: six dead (three Romanians and three Hungarians) and 278 wounded (190 Romanians and 88 Hungarians), a large number of devastated buildings and, above all, a violent psychological shock for a region of people used to serene cohabitation who had no idea that such extreme circumstances could befall them.

These events make up one of the blackest pages of the post-revolutionary period. They were a grave warning to make us understand where chauvinistic propaganda, irresponsible provocations, senseless rigidities, intolerance, refusal of inter-ethnic exchange, incitement to vengeance and acts of vendetta can lead. On that occasion, I loudly and strongly restated my conviction that problems can only be resolved through calm discussion. I asked both sides to show restraint and to not give in to their compulsions in order to avoid irresponsible provocations – even verbal ones. I told everyone that having an attitude of firm principle and restraint also includes respecting one another and making the effort to understand other people's interests in order to come up with fair and reasonable solutions by way of negotiation and mutual compromise, through respect of the fundamental principles of a democratic society and a Constitutional State. This is the only possible way to meet the demands of the minorities who were mistaken in believing that they could impose solutions through force and violence. I unequivocally condemned all forms of extremism and excess which were harmful to Romanians and Hungarians, both concerned above all with building a democratic society representing the necessary framework needed to better resolve the questions before us.

Some people reproached us – both the Provisional Council for National Unity and me personally, who was president of the council – for not having resorted to force in order to avert and disarm the conflict. To, thus, accuse us is to forget the context we were in, the tension that reigned throughout the country, the fact that the power structures were still provisional and the lack of a reliable and efficient police force. These forces were unorganized, fearful, hesitant and very unsure for reasons already mentioned and were not in a position to face such serious situations. It is also true that after thoroughly examining all aspects of the question, I was led to believe that the use of force could have had even worse consequences, even provoking an escalation with unforseeable results, the risk of an inter-ethnic war not being excluded. This would not only have been a catastrophe for the entire country, but also for the entire region and possibly even for all of Europe. We were in a void from the point of view of national security, suspended in an unstable geopolitical context and subject to an extraordinary domestic and foreign pressure.

Finally the path of discussion and negotiation paid off and the committee appointed by the Provisional Council for National Unity succeeded, after much difficulty, in reestablishing order in Târgu Mures and reaching compromises satisfactory to all parties involved. This opened the door for negotiations on the election of local authorities, and little by little, life went back to normal.

These dramatic events tarnished the image of Romania and the new power, groundlessly accused of having organized a "pogrom of the Hungarian minority" with the Securitatea's help, which was supposedly back in operation. It is easy to imagine what the foreign media would have said if we had reestablished order by force! Once established, it is difficult to change and correct this image about which we can unmistakably say that it is at the very least, tendentious and malevolent. The Târgu Mures conflict offers a distressing example of the way in which the media is able to completely twist information in order to deceive the public. Seriously beaten by Hungarian demonstrators, a Romanian, Mihaila Cofariu, will remain disabled for life; this lynching was caught on video by an Irish cameraman who immediately broadcast the images throughout the entire world, claiming that Mihaila Cofariu was a Hungarian demonstrator, a victim of the Romanians, thus reinforcing the thesis of an anti-Hungarian pogrom. Those who hastened to broadcast these images accompanied by false commentary never bothered to recognize their error and to reestablish the truth.

The tragic events of March 1990 in Târgu Mures were harmful to everyone. It was difficult for us to resume talks with the representatives of the Hungarian community, but it was the only way to come to a fair and reasonable decision. Little by little, street confrontations were replaced by those that take place within the frameworks of democratic institutions, where we can and have to confront the diverging interests of different social categories groups. Even if Romania was, at first, incapable of avoiding outbursts, it eventually succeeded in controlling the nationalistic conflicts to preserve order within the country while respecting the rights and liberties of all its citizens. All of this occurred in a trouble zone at a moment when Eastern Europe was already beginning a process of disintegation, with the tragic consequences we had experienced and dangers I feared not everyone had yet assessed.

University Square

T he first free elections were sceduled to take place on May 20. The Târgu Mures conflict had exploded two months prior to the day. April 20 marked the first day that the "University Square" movement began; a handful of apparently heterogenous elements took possesion, in the name of freedom and democracy, of a fairly large surface area in the center of Bucharest to hold an open forum for the struggle against what they called "neo" and "crypto" communism. Banners, grafitti, loud-speakers, posters, leaflets, even a balcony from which speakers took turns professing their democratic faith... nothing was missing from this movement which formed during a very aggressive electoral demonstration of the National Christian and Democratic Farmers Party. A few people present had the idea to occupy this central point in Bucharest and to make a grand display of permanent unrest. I could not see the need for this or how it added to the political evolution of a country which, after years of dictatorship and then the turmoil of the Revolution, overwhelmingly desired to strengthen the Constitutional State and the democracy to assure politcal stability – indispensable for the proper development of economic reforms intended to establish a market economy at a tolerable rate for the entire population.

Like always, I wanted to know who these demonstrators were and what they wanted. I quickly realized that these questions were not that easy to answer.

Was this a foreign provocation? This was of little importance in so far as such acts remain unproductive as long as

domestic sociological realities do not offer them a favorable environment in which to expand. I was trying to understand the precise deep causes of miscontent, the com-
bination of interests which was pushing several thousand
individuals to turn their backs on a rather encouraging political development. Apparently, the demonstrators who
were occupying the square day and night had very diverse
motivations and their joint emotional platform which de-
scribed the square as a "neo-communist free zone" was too
vague to satisfy me. This was also mentioned in an am-
mendment proposed by the National Liberal Party, member of the Committee for the elaboratation of the electoral
law, taken up again in a text called the "Timisoara
Proclamation" before becoming one of the slogans of the
University Square demonstration. How could I not see in
this a deliberate desire to raise doubts about the elections
scheduled to take place? How could I not question the democratic convictions of these people who claimed to decide, in advance and on their own accord, the limits of national sovereignty?
Certainly, this time it was much more difficult to believe
that it was a spontaeous uprising as similar demonstrations were taking place almost at the same time in
Belgrade, Sofia and other capitals of ex-Eastern bloc countries. Without attempting to look past what would give me
an immediate political result, I also had to take into account the foreign media movement which played on people's sympathy and which was aimed at deluding the defenders of liberty and democratic values.
There were misfits there, those uncontrollable people who
lend a hand in any street demonstrations without any con-

cern for its political purpose. They had already proved their defiance of all established order and shown a tendency toward anger and the expression of their opinions through violence. There were also radicals there, the "jacobins" who would have voluntarily thrown themselves in front of tens of thousands of people and their weapons. Another category of idealistic politicians wanted a "permanent revolution." This revolutionary sect was made up of a kind of militant fascists.

There were also a lot of students. They were expressing an extreme unwillingness to compromise with the values of their parents' generation. Still naive and lacking political experience, they believed they were participarting in a movement which would cause a break with the hated past and bring about true social renewal.

The intellectuals, sometimes of high standing, who were supporting this movement without always mingling with the demonstrators and without getting close enough to know them better and analyze their plans and ambitions, wanted to make up for not having protested during the more perilous conditions of the dictatorship with this extremism. Others took it upon themselves to create a moral renaissance which I wasn't sure that all strata of the population needed; no one knows the exact cost of the sorrow and suffering which every individual experienced during the historic catastrophe of the last few years. Some intellectuals who had given up their duty to society during the dictatorship were more vehemently feeling the need for redemption, a less evident need for other parts of the population who had freed themselves from their tasks without betraying themselves.

Politicians handicapped by their small constituency also used this platform to pass along a message whose content did not worry me; I was certain that it was far from what the country expected of us.

In fact, it didn't take me long to realize that this heterogeneous movement was not politically based on a social reality which fundamentally questioned our choices. Just the opposite, it exasperated the majority of people who were eager to finish with problems and start legitimizing a government capable of working on the country's economic recovery through free elections.

By waiting, I was trying to find openings and common ground to diffuse the crisis through discussion and compromise. I was convinced that in a still fragile social and political context, any show of force could poison events, making the conflicts more difficult to resolve and provoking violent, uncontrollable reactions.

I asked some members of the Provisional Council for National Unity to organize a meeting with the demonstrators' representatives. I wanted to have a real political dialogue, to listen to their opinions and their demands, then try to explain our point of view to them and find some common ground. Apparently, this desire to have a discussion was not shared, and I began to ask myself questions about the sincerity of people who wanted democracy without elections and power without discussions.

Finally, the delegation which was formed preposed the precondition that all dicussions take place live on television, either at University Square itself, or at the Parliament building. I refused this demand, concerned with avoiding outbursts and not wanting to open up the possibilty for disorder which, I knew, if ever it came to that, would be very difficult for me to control.

Later on, I regretted my refusal; at the close of such a confrontation, I would certainly have rounded up a larger amount of support for my political actions when compared with a such a confused protest, expressed by a minority totally cut off from the real feelings of the country. In fact, what exactly were they protesting?

My analysis leads me to believe that behind its revolutionary form, behind its popular appearance, in the incoherence of its opinions, they were refusing precisely the societal choice that Romania had made. The refusal to recognize the legitimacy of the election results proved it. Once again, this movement was not the true "opposition;" the real one existed within the Provisional Council for National Unity, a kind of improvised parliament where all opinions could be expressed, where points of view were exchanged and debates took place directly in front of television cameras, and most importantly, where we were laying the foundations for a future elected parliament. The University Square movement – which I know beyond a doubt was not organized by students as their associations left the movement immediately after the elections – was the radical denial of the democracy which was coming to power.

I am convinced that the manner in which the opposition wanted to exploit this demonstration, the fact that they encouraged it in order to exert political pressure unfair to the true opposition taking place within the framework of fledgling institutions, was flagrant proof of duplicity and a total lack of sincerity. The National Salvation Front's success in the May elections (65% of the votes) and my own personal success (85% of the votes) can also be explained by the rejection of the anarchist movement, an instable factor of psychological pressure. The electorate was wary of the troubles created in the name of the desire for social peace, stability and democracy. The free vote was the guarantee that the national will could be freely expressed in favor of democracy and stability, a very necessary step on the road to structural reform.

Free Elections and Violent Protests

Through the May 1990 parliamentary and presidential elections, the Romanian people explicitly let their choices be known. These choices not only validated the policy led since December 1989, but also indicated in what direction they wanted us to go and at what pace. The National Salvation Front benefitted from the prestige of those who had directly participated in the Revolution and the spectacular results obtained over such a short time span. In addition, its reform programs were clear and unambiguous. On the other hand, the opposition parties, especially those which had supported the University Square movement, seemed more fond of violent protests than concerned with the construction of a credible and constructive alternative.

After the May 20 elections which gave Romania a legitimate power structure, I was twice reproached concerning my attitude toward the University Square demonstrators. Refusing to accept the leaders which emerged from the ballot box, these people were continuing their movement and demanding my head as the President elected with 85% of the vote. This minority, which judged itself above the "thoughtless mass of voters," made a mockery of the popular will and of most fundamental democratic rules. This did not seem to bother some very eager human rights defenders who, especially overseas, gave an inaccurate image of Romania, probably without realizing that by discouraging economic aid from industrialized countries they were prolonging the suffering of a people who, through their vote, had simply expressed their desire for democracy, social peace and stability.

Some people reproached me for not having immediately terminated this movement as the voters had willfully elected me as the legitimate President. The new government and myself were accused of weakness. These demonstrators had not respected the election rules and had spread their political message in any way they liked. After having listened to them, the voters had expressed a different choice. The democratic pact now demanded that they end a movement which clearly went against the popular will. Their refusal to recognize the ballot's verdicts rightfully called for a police intervention to put an end to their actions which challenged the officials whom the country had freely chosen.

Deciding to intervene in this way was not something we wanted to decide hastily; we didn't want to humiliate them and add to their electoral defeat by making them submit to the force of those who had won. I was counting on the protesters' good sense. Indeed, having understood the lesson of free elections, a good number of them had left the square and the movement was running out of steam. In the end it seemed safer to me to let it die naturally.

I was also reproached for the June 13 intervention when I accepted the government decision to use the police to restore University Square, the heart of Bucharest, back to normal. I did it because there was only a handful of remaining demonstrators and because the government had reached an agreement the night before with the ones on a hunger strike on the lawn of the National Theater.

Though I wholeheartedly believe in the principle of this evacuation, I admit that the way it was carried out left much to be desired. The few diehards who were still there were dislodged in the early morning without any resistance and without provoking reactions from the people present or the passerbys. Nevertheless, to re-establish hygiene in this square which for nearly two months served as a dormitory, refectory, kitchen, bathroom, toilet, etc., city hall officials and health officials asked the policemen dispatched on the scene to deny people access for a few hours in order to carry out essential cleaning. It was a mistake. It wrongly implied that we wanted to prevent a new gathering. From there people extended this to feeling as if we were shackling freedom of expression and all liberty. This was all it took to once again add fuel to the fire.

On the morning of June 13, several groups of protesters invaded the area surrounding the square. Political forces which had poorly swallowed their electoral defeat wanted to take advantage of this unexpected occasion to attempt a coup just when the newly elected parliament was assembling.

Toward noon, the protesters attacked the police who were on the scene, inexperienced rookies from the police academy whom we had called upon because they were young and there was more of a chance that they would be seen favorably by a population still harboring very violent feelings toward the police of the old regime. Lacking the necessary equipment to defend themselves, not knowing how to properly make use of their weapons, this police force was quickly overrun and watched their cars be set on fire. Worse, Marian Munteanu, leader of the Student League – the group which had just left University Square – made a miraculous appearance, spoke to the crowd and claimed that the students arrested in the morning were being held by the police. Large numbers of them went to the police headquarters. The protesters invaded the building, beat up the people they found there, devastated the offices and ended up setting them on fire. Having found weapons, they took hold of them. There were gunshots fired and victims claimed. And they found no arrested students.

From there, a violent march which sacked everything in its path headed toward the nearby Interior Ministry. We had just enough time to take minimal resistance measures. Fire bombs were thrown and the flames spread upwards. Using some Public Works vehicles found nearby, the protesters tried to smash open the front door. Most upsetting was that they were trying to incite the military personnel of protecting the building to react. The Romanian Intelligence Service headquarters was also devastated and then, at the beginning of the evening, the protesters attacked television headquarters and turned the building upside down. The images which were coming to us live on television were unbearable. Their violence reminded me of the fascist rebellion of 1941.

On all of these occasions, the forces of order couldn't do anything because they lacked the means. In addition, it was psychologically difficult to ask the police, so soon after the Revolution, to confront an overexcited crowd.

Added to what we were already beginning to find out about the day's trying events, the sacking of the television building, which the entire country could follow live on their TV sets, provoked a certain panic. People were afraid to see the start of democracy threatened by blind violence and the election results questioned by the brutal force of a minority. I knew that despite its spectacular eruption, this marginal force did not represent a political danger. I did fear the reaction of those who were accusing the government of weakness which, backed up by an undeniable legitimacy, could demand a more authoritarian policy, supported by social forces which it would have been careless not to take advantage of. Yet, we had to be aware of the overwhelming responsibility on our shoulders; we didn't have the right to put the entire country in danger.

The Miners' Intervention

Scarcely a few months after a revolution which had completely turned the institutions upside down, and less than a month after the first free open elections, the new government did not yet have a structure capable of defending public order. It was in these conditions that the government had to face the events of June 13 and 15, 1990, when the police were finally called in to clear University Square. This provoked a particularly extreme reaction on the part of the movement's protagonists and sympathizers, who attacked the police and the headquarters of several State institutions with an unexpected ferocity. The country's capital was in the middle of a nightmare: a population terrified by scenes of violence and anarchy, the downtown ravaged by explosions and fires, wild gangs attacking police units...

To resolve this grave crisis which was once again making the specter of civil war appear, between a very active minority and those who were determined to defend what we had attained democratically through the elections, I saw it as my duty to use the authority I had gained through the May 20 vote. It was not exactly part of responsibilites, but after only three weeks since the elections, the new parliament still had not convened and the new government still had not been formed. We were, thus, in a momentary, but very real, power "halt". The State institutions were waiting for the newly elected parliament to begin managing the country and to put an end to this uncertain and provisional post-revolutionary period.

I, thus, spoke to the nation by radio and television asking them to defend the Constitutional State. My message was extremely clear: "A certain number of very violent individuals, armed with knives and Molotov cocktails, assaulted the police and seriously riled them up. They set fire to police vehicules, incited the population to violence and disorder, attacked and burned police buildings in the capital and the Interior Ministry and stole weapons. Institutions and shops have been devasted. The efforts of firemen and policemen to contain this devastating chaos remain fruit-less... It is clear now that it is an organized attempt to over-throw violently the government freely and democratically elected on May 20... In the name of the democracy brought to us through free elections, we ask all citizens of the capital to firmly refuse these irresponsible acts of vio-lence and to support the police in re-establishing peace and tranquility. We ask all conscious and responsible citi-zens to gather around the Government and television buildings to defend this democracy gained with so much difficulty..."

It was our duty to issue this call because the fundamental institutions of the State were in jeopardy. It was addressed to the population of Bucharest and I was surprised to hear that the miners from the Jiu Valley had decided to show up in the capital. Their coming seemed unnecessary to me, but I was not able to stop them – just as last time we were not able to stop them, one year later they returned, driven this time by social demands and determined to surpass the government's authority, who tried everything to stop them but in vain.

Power has no means to contain the movement of a crowd if it refuses to resort to violence. People still have trouble accepting this fact, but even Western countries, who have infinitely more efficient structures to respond to such out-bursts, lack "pacifistic" means to control violence. I was upset to observe in the commentary on these events that certain people voluntarily accept that a violent crowd can overthrow a legitimate power, but do not understand that this same power can have in turn its own fighters, equally difficult to control and subdue! During critical moments, the government's political reasoning has no more impact on its own supporters than it does on its adversaries. This leads me to believe that the authors of these commentaries would have prefered an armed intervention, unaware that this would only have amplified the disorder.

Unfortunately, we were not able to prevent the miners' violent acts, despite the call that I personally issued to them asking them to not respond to the provocations and to join with the police in order to help them restore order in the capital. They considered it their duty to not heed my request and to respond to the events of the night before by sacking the headquarters of the political parties of opposition. Others, wrongly considering the University and its students responsible for an attempted Coup d'Etat, wanted to reestablish order there. This regrettable attitude is above all due to the opinion expressed by part of the University Square movement, who, after the elections, let it be known that the popular masses, incapable of understanding democracy, had made a bad choice.

Fully regretting the brutalities committed, I can say today that the country has just come out of an extremely difficult ordeal. Five people were found dead the night of June 13, before the arrival of the miners.

Certain people reproach me for having thanked the miners on June 15 for their intervention, proof in their eyes that I had asked them to come, which began the rumor that I had requested they commit violent actions. I must say that the few words uttered on this occasion were above all aimed at convincing the miners to leave Bucharest and to dissolve the "popular militia" which they wanted to substitute for the police to reestablish public order.

Our political adversaries, of course, tried to take advantage of this by accusing us of having wanted to terrorize them. I cannot find one example, in the history of democracies, of a power that wanted to consolidate an evident electoral victory by the use of force. The Romanian political opposition did not prove to be on the level by its analysis of the events and by the image it gave to a country whose interests it claimed to protect.

Despite what had occurred, a bridge was crossed.

The elections had set the political chessboard in place and given the government the legitmacy it needed in order to tackle fundamental problems. The failure of the University Square movement discouraged those who were hoping to obtain political benefits through disorder and violence and awarded us a climate of relative stability. The newly elected bicameral Parliament took charge of the country's concerns and established a new Constitution. The President elect was able to give his speech and take his oath in front of Parliament. The President proposed that Mr. Petre Roman be given the responsibility of constituting a new cabinet; this proposal recieved the vote of confidence from Parliament, whose two houses would also later approve the government program.

I must specify that despite the comfortable majority obtained in the two houses by the National Salvation Front (65%), I proposed, as President of the Republic, that the opposition parties participate in the government. They refused to do so, partly because the National Salvation Front had the majority at its disposal which gave it sole governing capabilities, and also because, in their opinion, it was wiser that the opposition keep its critical position. In addition, because of possible social difficulties, the opposition found it more advantageous not to take on any government responsibilities.

Nevertheless, all parliamentary groups were proportionately represented in the two-house system, in the offices and in the committees – which allowed us to work in harmony with the country's political groups. I was also committed to carrying out my duties in direct and continual conjunction with all political groups. I regularly informed the leaders and heads of parliamentary groups about important questions and consulted them about all problems of general interest.

We had entered into a new stage of our political life: the structuring of the Constitutional State in which the Parliament, elected by free vote, was put in charge of establishing a new Constitution, the principal objective of the government being the institution of economic reform.

In Search of Balance and Stability: Structuring the Constitutional State

The End of Provisional Power

The May 20, 1990 parliamentary and presidential elections confirmed the democratic choices of the December Revolution. They gave power to the majority which had stepped forward and ended an unstable period when the political forces still had not received the legitimacy of the vote. Romania finally had revived a democratic tradition interrupted for half a century.

In my nomination speech on June 20, I was anxious to remind everyone that our principal mission was to take action on the Revolution's goals. I hoped that the goals could be the base of a national reconciliation, perhaps still difficult to envision, but necessary for the balance and stability that the government needed in order to undertake the reforms desired by all of Romanian society. I insisted that the confrontation of opinions and interests should leave the street and be set within the framework of institutions, from now on capable of housing a political battle respectful of democratic rules and an adversary that we assumed would be motivated by the same desire.

We had to draw up the plan for a new Constitution based on agreed-upon principles, among them the legislative role and control of Parliament, the respect for citizens' fundamental rights and liberties guaranteed by a strong and independent judiciary. It was clear to us that this text should be one for the entire country and we immediately did everything possible so that the parliamentary opposition could participate in the creation of the text.

Economic reform is a much longer and difficult process. First of all, a certain number of legislative provisions should institute the economic and financial conditions of the market economy. We also had to transform the State economic institutions into commercial companies with public capital and to simplify their functions to give them real autonomy in a competitive market. Privatization should start with small and medium-sized enterprises. Removing price controls should complete this first phase of measures, without forgetting an adequate taxation of revenues and turnover and social protection legislation which would be in a position to settle work conflicts, to assure the right to strike, to make union activity possible and so on. As a general rule, we had to allow private citizens to take on a certain number of responsibilities which had been previously confiscated by the State.

Concerning agriculture, the farmers should be able to decide for themselves the forms of organization and production desired, which called for a preliminary distribution of land.

The newly elected Parliament and the Government were, thus, confronted with multiple and urgent problems. They had to carry out a complete transformation of Romanian society, by taking into account our economy's possibilities, without compromising the country's social and political stability, while also trying to control inflation and unemployment. The Government's and Parliament's social policy endeavored to carry out the changes without conflict and tension.

It seemed indispensible to me to stop my speech on the moral aspects of our policies and to also specify the direction which we wanted the transformations to take; the State would serve the citizens, which implies a reduction of the political and economic pressure from public authorities over the individual. Administrative decentralization and privitization in the economic domain make up the indispensable conditions for this to take place. But it was also necessary to bring back the work ethic which the old regime had caused to disappear and without which social progress was inconceivable. I was persuaded that our only chance was to put our principal assets forward: creative intelligence, intellectual ability, the enterprising spirit, committment and a sense of moderation – traits specific to our people.

Such a program of democratization of society also calls for the respect of the fundamental rights and liberties of all citizens, including those belonging to ethnic, national and religious minorities. I specified that in this domain, we would respect the principles expressed in the program of the Revolution (especially that which defined Romania as a national unified State in the territory where many minorities lived), international regulations and the practices of a democratic State. The automatic presence of minority representatives in the Parliament proved our desire to completely integrate minorities into the country's political structure.

The 1989 Revolution and the May 1990 elections also satisfied our goal to participate in the construction of Europe in the same way as other countries, with whom we intended to be equal partners. Despite the vicissitudes of recent history, Romania is a latin European country. It is today rediscovering the universal values of European civilization, which have always been a part of Romania and of which we have amply participated in in the past.

I hope that the opinions and suggestions of my nomination speech were significant guide marks to help accomplish the Revolution's goals. It is true that the two years I had provided for was a very short amount of time and also ran the risk of being too dense compared to all that I wanted to accomplish: to strengthen the fundamental balance of the country, achieve social peace and stability, to get the Constitutional State functioning and to give the population the responsibilties which had been taken away from them. It is was clear to me that this period of transition would be full of obstacles and snares and that we all had to show alot of flexibility and tact in order not to threaten progress by untimely impatience. At any time, unforseen upheavals could call everything back into question and I had the choice between going slowly to not jeopardize the still fragile democracy, or to accelerate the movement to quickly pass up the point of no return. Romanian society was still at the boiling point and I had every reason to fear political turmoil and social danger. I was nonetheless persuaded that it was necessary to enact structural reforms as quickly as possible to give Romania the chance to participate in Europe's renewal process.

The Government at Work and
New Social Tensions

After the May 1990 elections, Petre Roman, who had led the provisional Government until this date, was placed in charge of forming the new cabinet, a move which had received Parliament's vote of confidence. I was assuming that once the cabinet was in place, things would go back to normal. It was a young and dynamic government team and conclusively proved from the very start its desire for change and the firmness with which it intended to enact the fundamental reforms that everyone was expecting.

We must recognize that the government worked in difficult conditions, as much within the country as outside of it. In the country itself, the government's economic supports were disappearing at the same time that the institutions and specific mechanisms of the centralized economy were collapsing, without the fledgling market economy providing it with some new ones. Outside the country, the economic collapse of the COMECON countries, especially the Soviet Union, the Gulf crisis, the embargo on Libya and on the former Yugoslavia, deprived us of our energy resources and of important markets at a moment when the global economic crisis had taken on worrying proportions. In addition, in its transactions with international banking and financial authorities, Romania was at a disadvantage, paradoxically because of the fact that it did not have a foreign debt (it even had a foreign trade surplus); in a period of crisis, lending organizations prefer to handle old customers and hesitate accepting any new ones. Thus, while countries whose foreign debt was already considerable could obtain sizeable loans in two years time, all of Romania's loan requests were being turned down.

Though domestic economic disasters and foreign problems were getting worse, the Romanian government still had the courage to start radical reform which excluded all steps backward. Though the reforms were undeniably necessary, some possibly should have been staggered over time to allow the government to better coordinate them to avoid overwhelming social effects. The population did not always fully understand.

The Prime Minister and Economic Reforms Minister, perhaps, did not have a clear enough vision of the reforms' consequences on the macro and microeconomic levels. They spontaneously enacted measures provoking conflicts with unions, Parliament and finally even with their own parliamentary group which asked several times for a precise reform program and a reasonable timetable for its implementation with detailed indications concerning the legislative provisions to be taken. The Government refused to provide it, preferring to see in the legislators' natural concern a "conservative" policy meant to hinder its action. The way in which the Government liberalized prices (October 1, 1990), arranged the convertibility of the national currency and dismantled several large industrial plants considerably worsened social tensions and weakened the national economy.

In the first months of 1991, criticism targeting Prime Minister Roman had multiplied and those who disagreed with his Governmental decisions had become more and more numerous and virulent.

As early as June, at the Prime Minister's suggestion, together we considered his possible resignation, principally with the prospect of broadening the government's political make-up. It was also a question of entrusting the leadership of this new cabinet to Teodor Stolojan. Today I regret not having made this decision earlier. It could have helped us avoid the conflicts which followed.

The August 19, 1991 coup d'état in Moscow shook the entire world and worried us tremendously. Informed of what was happening in Moscow and determined to keep Romania on the course it had chosen for itself and that no domestic political force had yet called into question, I immediately called a meeting of the High Defense Council to outline a strategy capable of facing any possible situation. I also called Prime Minister Roman, on vacation in Madrid, who surprised me by asking me if he should come back to Bucharest or not. I told him to come home as soon as possible and upon his arrival we had an interview during which he asked me to contact Mr. Ianaiev, leader of the coup, whom I had met in Prague during the signing of the treaty disbanding the Warsaw Pact, and who had met me at the airport during a official visit to Moscow when he was Vice-Prime Minister. I explained to my Prime Minister why such a step was inadvisable, and on August 20, Romania was one of the first countries to unequivocally condemn this coup d'etat attempt in a declaration of the High Defense Council which also specified that our country intended to continue down the road it had freely chosen. Our unanimous decision was firm, calm and clear.

We also hailed our brothers of the Republic of Moldova, whose political leadership condemned the Moscow rebels and took advantage of these circumstances to proclaim independence from the USSR on August 27, 1991. This was an important moment in the life of this Romanian territory, which had been swallowed by the Soviet Empire in June 1940 following the Molotov-Ribbentrop pact. Some believed that Romania should have acted to reunite Moldova with Romania, as this historic region had been pulled away from us fifty years earlier. This is an unrealistic position which does not take into account the European political situation and international conventions concerning borders established after World War II. Nor does it not take into account the feelings of this new republic's people. A more realistic and useful idea was to develop a natural relationship between the two States and to facilitate a general process of cultural and economic integration, with the hope of forming a common spiritual space, leaving it to History to find the solution of an obviously painful problem that would have been dangerous to try to resolve immediately.

At the end of the summer 1991 social tensions were becoming more worrisome every day, especially among the Jiu Valley miners.

I learned that the Lupeni miners had gone on strike, that it was taking on alarming proportions, that there would be a mass rally in Petrosani and that the demonstrators were asking the Prime Minister to come negotiate on the spot – which I advised him against, while recommending that he postpone his trip to Austria to be present for any developments in the situation.

The initial economic demands about salaries and work conditions at the Petrosani rally were quickly transformed into a political dispute, with the protesters demanding the

Government's resignation. The miners decided to go to Bucharest to impose their point of view by force. On the way, shops and the Petrosani railroad station were desvastated, several thousand miners blocked the trains and forced the engineers to head toward the capital, and those who tried to talk to them to convince them to change their minds – railroad officials, the prefect of Dolj, and the military commander of the Craiova garrison – were threatened and even beaten up.

Once in Bucharest, the miners occupied the square in front of Government Headquarters. They demanded that the Prime Minister come and negotiate with them on the spot, refusing to form a delegation to carry out negotiations under acceptable conditions. Attempting to attack the building, they were pushed back by the police. Not satisfied, they decided to invade Parliament the next day to also demand my resignation. The miners, to which uncontrollable gangs had been added – like always on such an occasion – succeeded in entering the Parliament floor to ask the deputies to relieve me of my duties.

This blunder was originally a meaningful political act. Refusing to let themselves be intimidated, a great number of deputies of all convictions explained to the crowd that we were in the middle of instituting a Constitutional State, with lawful mechanisms, and that Parliament did not have the right to dismiss a popularly elected President. Some having suggested that the only way would be that the President himself resign, the protesters headed toward Cotroceni Palace, seat of the President of the Republic.

I called together the members of the High Defense Council and the Government. Prime Minister Roman of-

My grandfather, my two cousins and myself — Oltenita — 1935

My mother, my father and myself — 1938

My three brothers in 1958 — from left to right: Mihai, myself, Crisan and Eugen

My wife Elena and myself — Bucharest — 1991

With my teachers and friends from S.P. Haret highschool — Bucharest 1969

With a friend in Sweden — 1969

International round-table discussion "Youth and European security" — June 1969 — Snagov
Directors of various european youth organizations

December 22, 1989

December 22, 1989

December 23, 1989

January 12, 1990

January 12,1990

January 12,1990

January 28, 1990

Visiting Nicolas Iorga's memorial house — August 1990

Electoral campaign 1990

Electoral campaign 1990

In Rome in 1991 with Jiri Pelikan (previous president of czechoslavachian television as well as the commission for foreigners during Prague spring in 1968)

In Rome with two young Italians

At the National Assembly in 1992

Discussion at the National Assembly in 1992

Crowd of people during the 1992 electoral campaign

Meeting for the electoral campaign of 1992

Inauguration of the French Cultural Center in Northern Romania — Iasi — 1993

Visit of a hydroelectric dam in Brazil

Summer 1992

fered his resignation, convinced at that moment that it was the only solution to diffuse the crisis, especially after our discussions in June. We all agreed to draw up a communiqué stating this. I asked the leaders of the various political groups to come and join me and I informed them of the Prime Minister's decision. Together, we discussed who could replace him at the head of the government. I also suggested that they participate in the meeting with the delegation of miners, which had finally been formed and whom I considered it would be a good idea to welcome; everyone found this to be a good idea but no one wanted to accompany me.

My September 27 discussion with the miners' representatives was recorded and later broadcast on radio and television. I did not miss the opportunity during the discussion to firmly condemn the miners' intervention and to resolutely explain to them that their demand to have the Prime Minister come to the strike site to negotiate was unreasonable, that the members of the Government had other more important things to do than to resolve the work conflicts of a particular company. I believe I succeeded in making them understand that a leadership change – Prime Minister or President – would not change the economic reality and that, except for the desire to question a reform they had all prayed for, they should accept the idea that our policy was responding to unavoidable economic demands. Thus, I diffused a conflict which had deeply troubled the entire country and which had, once again, prejudiced us on the international scene.

Afterwards, Prime Minister Roman's attitude surprised, saddened and disappointed me. He expressed doubts concerning the opportunity to welcome the miners' delegation and to sign a communiqué with someone who, in short, had acted by placing himself above the law – he was referring to Miron Cosma, leader of the miners. I am glad to note that my attitude enabled the resolution of a conflict which the Government and its Prime Minister had been incapable of averting, preventing, or resolving. Even worse, Roman had asked two days prior, that as the President of the High Defense Council, I declare a state of emergency; I refused. This would have meant calling in the army, to which we would have then given weapons, which could have had extremely serious consequences. This suggestion was irresponsible and dangerous.

Likewise, arguing that "giving up his mandate" did not mean resignation – a distinction which no one brought up during the discussions with the representatives of the various parliamentary groups concerning the formation of a new Government – Roman reproached me for not having asked for a parliamentary confirmation of his resignation. He was forgetting that the representatives of all the political affiliations which were participating in this discussion had been in unanimous agreement with the solution that Roman himself had proposed. And he was also forgetting that, constitutionally, the President of the Republic has the power to consent to a Government official's resignation.

I was also shocked by the duplicity of the National Democratic and Christian Farmers Party which was holding a convention at the moment and whose representatives applauded a miners' delegation led by its union leader. This just when, after the discussions that they had had with me, satisfied with the results gained, the miners had finally accepted to leave the city. Likewise, militants from the Civic Alliance – a supposedly apolitical organization – mobilized their forces to convince the miners not to leave Bucharest before having won my resignation. This same group which had one year before sharply condemned the miners' intervention which came to save the Constitutional State, were now praising them for their actions against the legitimate Government. I couldn't help noticing that such an attitude was not a lesson in democracy and civics, but moreover proved to be a big concern for the national interest.

As soon as Mr. Roman resigned from the Romanian government, I began discussions with representatives from all parliamentary parties and asked them to nominate a Prime Minister acceptable to everyone, capable of forming a coalition government. The people I spoke with showed a lot of imagination, even proposing the names of some generals and bishops. Teodor Stolojan's name ended up standing out. One of the people having elaborated the strategic plan of transition toward a market economy, he had initially been Minister of Finance under Petre Roman, then, President of the National Agence of Privitization. Accepted by all the parties, Mr. Stolojan formed his government with important politicians from four main groups: the National Salvation Front, the National Liberal Party, the Ecologist movement, and the Democratic Agrarian Party (the National Farmers Party refused to participate). This was a first step toward a greater commitment from political groups toward business management.

The Stolojan Government aimed to pursue economic reform, and once the new Constitution and laws concerning local, parliamentary and presidential elections were adopted, promised to attend to the smooth development of elections. The government succeeded in its plans, directing business with calm determination, avoiding pitfalls and skillfully preserving the country's fundamental balances. On the other hand, they did not succeed in stopping the decline of industrial production to reach "zero growth." In 1992, we recorded the worst downfall of industrial production ever (– 20%), a deterioration of buying power and a noticeable reduction in revenues.

Obligated to take unpopular but absolutely necessary measures, Mr. Stolojan knew to appear open and approachable, tackling the stickiest economic questions with a frankness which brought him respect from unions, the media, and the public. Everyone admitted that his participation on the radio and on television was dictated by the need to explain and never by a taste for the spectacular.

The New Romanian Constitution

The principal mission of the Parliament elected in 1990 was to create a new Constitution, which was, in itself, a real political learning experience for the deputies and the citizens.

A Committee of senators and Parliament members, which brought together the representatives of all parties and experts in constitutional law, took charge of establishing a plan for the Constitution. Several of them had previously participated in the creation of the electoral law of 1990, adopted by the Provisonal Council for National Unity and

already containing a certain number of constitutional provisions (form of the State and the Government, eligible
functions etc.). As President of the Provisional Council for
National Unity, I had myself benefitted from that experience where we had to go beyond the immediate concerns
to foresee the future, to set up our country with a long-
term plan.

For three months, this Committee studied vast amounts of
documents, including the Constitutions of different democratic countries and the old Romanian Constitutions. The
members of the Committee consulted many times with
specialists from other democratic countries. In October
1990, we organized the international colloquium "Present
Trends of Constitutional Law" in Bucharest in order to obtain the most complete image possible of the ideas and
concerns of the best specialists in this domain.

The Committee drafted a preliminary plan for the
Constitution which was published and submitted to the
popultation for observations, questions and critiques. Two
months later, Parliament, in its status as a Constituent
Assembly, begain examining the plan point by point. For
four months, the deputies examined almost one thousand
amendments. After having rewritten the text to best correspond with the deputies' resolutions, the Committee dis-
tributed the newly revised document before the recess so
that each delegate could think about it on his own time.
The new text was then discussed again for about two more
months, finally submitted to the Assembly for vote and approved by the majority of Parliament members.

Being constantly updated on the progress of the plan for
the Constitution through the press, which granted entire

pages to the topic and through television, which broadcast the parliamentary debates live, the citizens were kept fully informed about the project.

During this period I met legal experts from the European Council and international specialists who assured me that the plan for the Constitution conformed, in their opinion, to the democratic norms of modern States. They also considered that the procedures carried out for the drafting and the ratification of the text met the most scrupulous democratic demands and gave us the right to believe that the text approved by the December 8, 1991 referendum was indeed that which corresponded most closely to the desires of the entire population.

The December 8, 1991 referendum offered Romania a new Constitution. Through its spirit and its words, it gave concrete form to the goals of the December 1989 Revolution which aspired to make Romania a Constitutional State, where the system of checks and balances is respected, with a pluralistic and democratic government, and where the citizens freely choose representatives to exercise power in their name. The Constitution also stated, as did the National Salvation Front's December 22, 1989 Communiqué, that the Romanian economy would be a market economy with fair competition and that the State would assure social protection and economic development and guarantee non-violation of privacy. The State also defends the rights and liberties of individuals, everyone having the freedom to express his opinion. It assured that minorities have the same rights and liberties as everyone else, including the right to preserve, develop and express their ethnic, cultural, linguistic and religious identity within the framework of a united and indivisible State. The Constitution also provided that Romania must lead a good-neighbor policy of peace with the goal of European integration in mind, everything having the goal of the blossoming of the human being within the absolute respect of his rights and liberties.

The new Romanian Constitution confirmed and implemented the program announced in the "December 22 Communiqué". With this new Constitution, Romania crossed a threshold and entered a new stage where upheavals and earthquakes no longer threatened to drive it from its chosen path. It rejoined the ranks of modern democracies and Constitutional States which respect the international norms concerning fundamental rights and liberties.

Local Elections, the Split of the National Salvation Front and a Not So "Amicable" Divorce

Adopted by the December 8, 1991 referendum, the new Constitution allowed for the creation of administrative and local election laws. After their ratification, the government was able to organize, in February 1992, elections for municipal and communal councils.

A coalition of opposition parties headed a very virulent campaign trying to take advantage of the economic and social difficulties which they attributed to bad management of the National Salvation Front government. The Front itself was in crisis, torn between those who continued to have confidence in me and a fringe element regrouped around Mr Roman, who had become leader of the party at the moment when I was elected President of Romania and had left the leadership of that group.

Wrongly considering himself an expiatory victim of a political battle where he was sacrificed as Prime Minister in order for me to win the Presidency, Mr. Petre Roman abandoned himself to shocking political attacks toward the people who had led the country with for almost two years and whom he discovered after the fact to be "old communists" – something he had never noticed as long as he had shared power with them. I wanted an explanation from Roman to try and understand his surprising slide toward positions diametrically opposed to those he had previously defended. Roman disappointed me by letting me know that he doubted my chances in the election, which pushed him closer to the opposition that he was now hoping would win. Less disappointed to note my former Prime Minister's opportunism than his meager amount of political shrewdness, I accepted this not exactly "amicable" divorce which was going to divide the National Salvation Front. During the National Conference in March 1992, Roman tried to lead the party toward positions contrary to his natural beliefs, and to arbitrarily impose a political line not having anything to do with the fundamental choices of the group he was leading. Poorly taken, this pressure urged a majority of the party's members to quit Roman's group to form the Democratic National Salvation Front, which afterwards became the Social Democratic Party.

When a country recovers its democratic life after having a one party dictatorship for so long, ideological and political cleansing is natural, and the other groups weren't spared these kinds of problems either. The schism of the National Salvation Front baffled the voters and disturbed parliamentary activity, considerably delaying the creation and ratification of legislative and presidential election laws which we believed should have taken place at the same time as local elections, but which we were forced to put off for several months. This gut-wrenching battle cost us a lot of seats in the local councils, especially in the big cities. The opposition parties' "Convention," which was beginning to take on a structure and to conduct a more coherent policy, scored well, but did not surpass the National Salvation Front, by far the country's principal political group. This breakthrough in the local elections forced the opposition to get more involved in the country's management and to not only confront problems on the local level, but those we were facing on the national scale.

The Parliamentary and Presidential Elections

The Democratic National Salvation Front was not in an enviable position; it had to prepare what looked to be a difficult electoral campaign and to reform the essential local structures.

I agreed to run for President supported by this party. I knew that the electoral battle would be rough. Nearly the entire social fabric was in crisis. As for me, it was less about battling the other candidates than establishing a dialogue with the country in order to bring about acceptable solutions to the problems we were facing. I wanted to give confidence back to those who were losing patience and to keep the country moving straight ahead, which was bend-

ing on discovering the depth of the economic disaster inherited from the dictatorship and the enormous effort
needed to avoid an even more serious crisis. In short, the
social and economic situation was my most formidable adversary, all the more so since unproductive political dis-
putes were aggravating the country's suffering. At the
same time, it seemed unacceptable to me to make promises I knew I couldn't keep, or to offer miraculous solutions
which would not have lasted more than one day.

I intitled my program: "I believe in change for the better
for Romania." The analysis of the situation, the seriousness of the dangers which threatened us, but also my profound confidence in the chances at recovery spared me
from making populist or demagogic promises. I chose, instead, lucidity, having nothing else to offer in the immediate except rigor and effort. My program proposed "a strategy for change which modifies the national realities in a
profound and lasting way," to denounce pointless confrontations in favor of social harmony, to refuse violence
and make way for discussion, to construct rather than demolish.

It was clear to me that what was at stake in these elections
was not the victory of a particular political power, but the
direction of the transformations to come and the destiny of
a country and a people who desired a Constitutional State,
a modern democracy and the stability likely to open development up to them in agreement with contemporary scientific and technological progress, to offer them a chance to
catch up to developed countries and to be integrated into
the structures of the world economy. This requires a considerable effort, uniting all powers and all abilities, with ab-

solutely no partisan exclusion. A market economy has the advantage that it allows the spirit of enterprise to blossom for the collective well-being. The State being responsible for establishing the rules, it must make sure the law is respected and see to it that the rhythm of reform does not exceed the threshold of tolerance on the social level and that it does not endanger the fundamental balances of the State by high unemployment, excessive inflation and so on.

Effort, responsibility, trust.

A moral renaissance.

We were not only in the middle of an economic crisis but also a social one, affected by the revolutionary upheaval of the political and economic system which was bringing about a profound change in our values. In a society whose moral fiber was seriously damaged by decades of dictatorship, such large changes run the risk of making room for new forms of corruption and alienation. This is why I believed a true program of moral cleansing was necessary. In 1990, when I left the National Salvation Front to become President, I had hoped that this party might become a party of incorruptibles, the standard bearer of respect for the law, an exemplary force to impose the rules of the Constitutional State.

A definitive break with the past does not resolve economic and social problems. Just the opposite, it creates new ones, at first. And if economic recovery demands that all social forces particpate in the national effort, moral purification of society asks no less of them. As for the inherited problems, the transition adds new temptations and makes other forms of social harm appear such as corruption, illegal practices, tax evasion, etc. Likewise, we are paying the price for our new liberty with an explosion of criminal activity which is threatening people and property and which we must contain as soon as possible.

I am not one of those people who is convinced that the appearance of this "middle class" (which the country needs) must happen by way of the quick and excessive enhancement of a certain number of law-defying individuals. On the contrary, such attitudes run the risk of producing serious social tensions, demoralizing business owners who respect the rules of the game and finally rupturing the balances on a national level. I thought it my duty to immediately ask for more severe laws to do away with practices representing a real danger to the democracy and the State. The social protection that the State owes its citizens is not only related to solving economic problems and doing away with the prejudice the nation suffers because of defrauders. It is, also to a form of dignity where all citizens know they are equal before the law.

In fact, my program was formed around one simple, vital idea: build a Constitutional State concerned with the intellectual and material comfort of its citizens, to whom it guarantees rights and liberties as well as favorable conditions for the development of education, science and the humanities allowing everyone to cultivate their abilities and spirit of enterprise in a just and equitable society.

And in time, I will aim this development toward the prospect of natural integration into European and Euro-Atlantic structures.

The majority of Romanians voted in unequivocal favor of this political line. They perhaps preferred to put their trust in someone who would endeavor to do things calmly and who was concerned with preserving the country's fundamental balances, without excluding anyone, refusing on principle the partisan intransigence which seems to have been the electoral strategy of other presidential candidates. Since not one of the six other candidates surpassed the 50% barrier of the total number of votes cast, (I, myself, only received 48%), a second round of voting was organized to decide between the first two candidates. Running against Professor Emil Constantinescu who represented the Democratic Convention, I was re-elected with 62% of the vote. In turn, and in spite of the difficulties which I have already spoken about, the National Democratic Salvation Front won the legislative elections, receiving 29% of the vote. The Democratic Convention, which gathered together approximately 18 different political groups, received only 21% and the National Salvation Front about 10%. Since the rules of the electoral law refused a seat in Parliament to groups not having taken at least 3% of the vote, only eight groups were able to send representatives to Parliament. Mr. Câmpeanu's National Liberal Party, which had left the Democratic Convention after the local elections, like some other fairly politically important groups, did not succeed in finding a voice in Parliament; this was an advantage for less influential parties who had understood the value of forming common lists. Parliament is now made up of 13 different groups, among them the Democratic Union of Romanian Hungarians plus representatives from the thirteen ethnic minorities, each one automatically having a Parliamentary seat.

Through the redistribution of seats left open because of the numerous groups not having received at least 3% of the vote, the National Democratic Salvation Front – later to be-come the SDRP-which had won the elections, was awarded the greatest number of seats in the Senate and in the House of Deputies (34%). Nevertheless, no single political group had an absolute majority, which did not always sim-plify things, but which at least has the advantage of forcing everyone to continually look for alliances and compromis-es, and, thus, learn the useful experience of tolerance and democracy.

The Presidential Address

R omania had a new constitution which provided it with an indisputably legitimate government through local, legislative, and presidential elections. These elections also rebuked those who claimed that the Romanian people were not mature enough for democracy and were unfit to choose its path. My address, given October 30, 1992, dur-ing the inauguration ceremonies, discussed this topic.

I also pointed out that the election results forced the politi-cal forces to reconcile and collaborate to avoid a political impasse or chronic instability which could compromise the reform program desired by the people and that the new government should conduct itself with determination, strengthened by its legitimacy.

After the experiences and hesitations during the three years since the Revolution, it was clear that reform could not be improvised. We needed to establish the theoretical and strategic foundations of the transition in the long-term and short-term government programs; we needed "A Global Plan of Re-structurization and Development."

Convinced that in this transition period, the self-regulation of the economy by market forces was absurd since these forces still did not exist, the government needed to enact efficient price supports allowing it to intervene in the national economy's management, re-structurization, and development. This would allow us to initiate, coordinate, and supervise the transition process (privatization, development of the private sector, State investments, etc.), set up a financial branch, increase the efficiency of resources and follow the economic indicators day by day in order to be able to intervene at the least sign of emergency. We could not forget the need for social protection, which the State should assure by working closely with the unions and employers and which remains an indispensable condition for reform.

In a transition period such as this, one must find a delicate balance between the State intervention in the economy and lack of involvement in a market system which must function according to the rules of private enterprise. Without being a substitute for economic factors and without discouraging the enterprising spirit with a overly heavy taxation, and not allowing itself to spend excessively which runs the risk of either aggravating inflation or increasing the public debt, the State should ensure domestic stability and lawful order, protect private and public property, preserve and manage the National estate and stop corruption. Economic recovery is impossible in a climate of insecurity and instability. The State should also create an institutional framework, a banking and financial system and a favorable climate for business, simplifying formalities and bureaucratic proceedings as much as possible, especially for those who take responsibility for public enterprise and should, thus, enjoy total autonomy.

It is, perhaps, a good idea to recall that in such a period of turbulence, the State must also remedy the inherent problems involved in the radical transformations which all of the social and economic systems are simultaneously undergoing. It must guarantee the supply of food and heat in winter and subsidize the sectors and branches where scarcity could cause dangerous social problems. It is also responsible for creating jobs and protecting disadvantaged workers with a guaranteed minimum wage, retirement and social aid, and for providing all citizens with medical assistance and the access to education. To contest the role of the State today, as certain people are taking it upon themselves to do, is to forget its responsibility concerning national culture, essential research, environmental protection and defense.

The idea is certainly not to return to the methods of a centralized economy, but to direct the process toward a market economy and to maintain, using the appropriate tools, the fundamental State balances; these balances cannot be ruptured without putting democracy itself in danger and can even jeopardize the direction of the transformations in progress.

At first, only the State is in a position to carry out the structural modifications likely to direct the national centralized economy towards a market economy, especially when it comes to setting up the still inexistant infrastructures in the private sector and stimulating the priority industries by favoring investments, State as well as private, domestic as well as foreign. Nevertheless, the State's strategy centers around reducing its participation in the economy and giving up the management of economic industries. Likewise, the broader integration of our economy into the world economy and international structures and systems requires us to adapt our economic and financial mechanisms, which the State must modify so that they are compatible with those of our partners, without forgetting to protect national interests.

My nominational address also allowed me to warn the government how arduous its task was and that the future of Romanian society depended on its success. I asked the parliamentary opposition to consider the particular situation Romanian society was in and, without renouncing their point of view, to support governmental action through constructive political activity, in a common effort to come out of this difficult period.

The urgence and importance of taking certain measures was such that it would have been desirable for parliamentary activity to be freed of tactical obstructions which had no regard for the country's interest. I also believe that such a policy would not have been a good idea for the electoral plan. The citizens proved that they understood the difficulties at that time and were ready to confront them and pay the price of reform. They also understood that this could not be done without effort, social discipline, an enterprising spirit and responsibility on all levels. In this effort for recovery, we cannot count on foreign aid, as important as it is, but must rely on our own strengths which would be a shame to waste by gratuitous protest and pernicious absenteeism. In order to catch up with developed countries, we must work like them and also adopt their organization and production. This is what Romania needs in the years to come.

Dialogues and Political Contacts

The elections changed our political makeup. Since no single group had obtained an absolute majority, a one-party government was impossible and it seemed reasonable to attempt to form an alliance capable of constituting a stable parliamentary majority.

A month of negotiations did not get me through people's hesitancies and evasions of one kind or another, which were not supported on matters of principle but aimed sorely at political maneuvering. I started by proposing what seemed the most natural to me in these very difficult conditions, namely a government of national unity. It would mean establishing a simple common program and a form of government acceptable by all. The majority of parties rejected this idea.

I, then, more modestly aimed to forge a simple coalition of several parties capable of giving the government a comfortable majority and securing a stability that the country sorely needed. This, also, would have given the majority of Romanians the feeling that, in the given conditions, the different political parties were conducting a common and necessary economic policy, led by a coalition government accepted by the opposition.

The Democratic Convention, the principal consolidation of the opposition parties, and the National Salvation Front refused this proposal, asking that the victorious party take charge. I reminded them that no one had won the elections since no party had had even a slight majority, but my argument did not convince those who seemed too embittered by their electoral defeat to recognize the similarities in our agendas and how, together, they could form a governmental foundation without anyone disowning the essence of their beliefs. It's too bad because the country would have been the winner.

I then suggested a government composed of technocrats. The leaders of several parties opposed this idea; they claimed that the principal political difficulties we were in the middle of confronting demanded a governmental response which gave the responsibility to a single party. In fact, in a moment of candor, Corneliu Coposu, president of the National Farmers Party (the most important opposition party), admitted to me that he did not intend to participate in a government whose failure was apparent because of the difficulties it faced. He found it wiser to remain on the sidelines and to reap the political rewards that would come from such difficulties. This is also the reason why he rejected the idea of a technocratic government, which would have served to shield the leading political group, which he preferred to see fail after having taken on sole governmental responsibilities.

Finally, I had the idea to propose a method which had proved effective in Spain, where after Franco's fall, the principal political forces had signed the Moncloa Pact; based on a basic program, it insured a sufficiently precise government framework which was agreed-upon to avoid troubles in any politically or socially dangerous period. The few principles around which I was hoping to establish consensus should not have posed any problems of conscience to the any of the groups as they had voiced these same principles in their platforms: bolster the democracy in the social and political domains, perfect economic reform which would assure a transition towards a market economy while trying to reduce the social cost as much as possible, pursue a realistic foreign policy toward our neighbors and strengthen ties with the West. Once again, the opposition parties were very suspicious, apparently unwilling to commit themselves in writing to a text which only restated the terms of their own electoral platforms.

A work group was nevertheless formed under the leadership of Adrian Nastase which started drawing up such a pact. These negotiations eventually fell through.

There came a time when these negotiations, which had gone on too long, had to end, if only to comply with the legally-imposed time limit. Nothing is more harmful to a country than prolonging a transitory political situation. After a certain amount of time, what starts out as the desire to be open can appear as a sign of weakness and evasion compared with the responsibilities we face. I regretfully noticed that the different opposition groups had no real desire to participate in any way with the formation of a parliamentary majority committed to supporting the government policy which had to design economic reform and insure the country of the political stabilility and social peace they desired. I, thus, asked the National Democratic Salvation Front, the group which held the majority of Parliament seats, to alone assume the responsiblity of forming a government made up of competent people, whether they belonged to the party or not, keeping in mind the opinions of the groups which were prepared to support the government politically. Some opposition parties were committed to having a constructive parliamentary attitude, thus giving the new government the break it needed to pass through the immediate difficulties, especially those of the approaching winter.

Aware of the trying sacrifices that the government had to ask of the country, in a political context where an absolute majority was not assured in the two houses, conscious also of the fact that the biggest of the government's problems was economic and linked to the reform that it was supposed to carry out, the National Democratic Salvation Front nominated Mr. Vacaroîu, an economist, to head the government, a person belonging to no single party and chosen uniquely because of his technical capabilities, especially his financial skills and his experience managing macro-structures. His close collaboration with the former Prime Minister, at whose side he had worked on the the elaboration of the transition strategy towards a market economy, had given him considerable experience as a statesman.

In the conversations and contacts that I had at this period, as I had continually done since the first days of the Revolution and afterwards within the framework of Provisional Council for National Unity, I attempted to instill a climate of trust and cooperation, listening to the other parties with sincerity and openly tackling all of the questions they asked me. There are situations where I know from the first instant that I will succeed in getting along with people whom I am meeting for the first time. This is my attitude toward my political adversaries, whom I do not see as enemies, especially when it comes to national interest, but as discussion partners to exchange ideas and opinions with, always useful even if we have different points of view.

Economic Reform

A Weighty Heritage

Except for a few differences, all the "real socialist" countries inherited the same economic disaster, no longer hidden behind an ideological curtain and staring us right in the face. The difficulties of the transition to a market economy show us, everyday, what we are capable of and we must make a conscious effort to accept even it's traumatic implications.

The former German Democratic Republic (East Germany) is a case in point. The 150 billion or so deutschmarks invested since 1989 to re-attach this country – perhaps the most economically efficient in the entire ex-Soviet block – to the economic and social structures of the reunited Germany (which weakened not only the German economy but also that of the entire European Community), seem insufficient. It is just one particular case anyway, since the other Central and Eastern European countries have not benefited from such an infusion of cash. Everyone tries to pull through for the better and to overcome in his own way the problems encountered on the road to transition. Romania, too, whose development is an example of the journey taken by all the other countries who are changing from a centralized economy to a market economy. The reasons which incited us to overthrow the totalitarian regime through a violent and amazing spasm, today give our efforts at recovery an altogether visible and exemplary character.

The Soviet economic model that all the so-called "socialist" countries adopted willingly or forcibly after the war was utopian and closely linked to a political system, depriving it of any "return" which would have allowed it to adapt itself according to practical results. It suffered, also, from a certain number of structural deficiencies that the Romanian political leadership aggravated by so faithfully following it.

We can blame first of all a pernicious authoritarianism, less for its excessive State control (as it was also the case elsewhere) than for its total contempt for reality. Decisions were made with the conviction that economic reality should, in one way or another, bend itself to them. Absolutely refusing to take into account practical results and to correct plans according to them, Romania's political leadership reached a point where what was thought at the top had nothing to do with what was really going on. It was a kind of economic schizophrenia made possible by a political despotism which had suppressed all means of social input and as a consequence deprived itself – it did not feel the need for it anyway – of feedback enabling it to measure the effectiveness of its choices.

The top leadership believed that political initiative could make up for economic effectiveness. They were too confident of the advantages of the system of socialist countries whose economic decisions were subordinate to political interests. Concerned over the country's total economic independence, Romanian leaders wanted to develop all sectors of industry without taking into account the energy and the available raw materials on the national level and the markets for these products, sure that they could always sell off the national production thanks to political intervention.

Paradoxically, the result was exactly the opposite: the Romanian economy became a machine which today, because of the changes the world has undergone, can no longer operate for lack of energy and for lack of an adequate supply of raw materials. In any case, it produces goods which the domestic market only needs a fraction of, and which are not competitive on the free international market.

Nothing proves perhaps in a more eloquent manner the dangers of a State-run economy and a State-run political system than to note that while Romania inherited the most rigid and inefficient system of Eastern European countries, it was the first country of the ex-Soviet block to open itself up and to develop positively.

At the beginning of the 1960's, in fact, Romania tried to have the Soviet economic model changed and to adapt itself to the laws of the market. Exchanges of every kind with the West (especially France, England and Germany) were considerably intensified at the time. A certain spirit of initiative in industrial development was felt. A post-university institution of learning specialized in management even trained a new kind of company boss. Romania was also one of the first Eastern countries to promote computer science by founding the Central Computer Science Institute which instigated application on the national economic level, with the goal of creating a uniform computer system – the departmental centers having the task of connecting all the important enterprises to a national network. In short, Romanian society seemed to be heading down a rather liberal road, as far as could be permitted in the given conditions.

Unfortunately, the intervention of Soviet and Warsaw Pact armies in Czechoslovakia in August 1968 was, for Eastern Europe, what the intervention of Russian armies had been against the 1848 revolutions: a sudden halt to any positive development, the road open now to the most inept political forces.

In only a few years, all the system's doors were closed and bolted down, and a country which we can truly say was at the avant-garde of changes happening in the East, was now the victim of a backpedaling policy in all the sectors of social and economic life and brought to the edge of a regression as amazing as the fervor which earned the reputation as the most turbulent of the Soviet block. The bureaucratic centralization, the State's pretentiousness to control and direct all sectors of economic life, paralyzed it. The spirit of enterprise and the force of inventiveness were squashed, resources were wasted in a way as irrational as ineffective, and, in short, economic activity was turned away from its natural mission, namely, to satisfy the needs of the people. Serious imbalances appeared in agriculture, whose natural trading channels were broken off; industrial branches of the manufacturing industry reached gigantic proportions, the energy shortage was considerably agravated, the development of the tertiary sector was neglected, if not outright abandoned. Result: the Romanian economy lost its competitiveness and was isolated from the global network.

The structural defects of the Soviet-style economic system, aggravated by those of a political system whose cult of personality was its expression, led Romanian society to economic disaster. It placed the country in a worse position than those of other Eastern European countries, who still managed to preserve a degree of openness and relative flexibility which was certainly beneficial. Worse, Ceaucescu's megalomania, which disguised itself as national independence, made him feed the dream of an autarchic economy, which not only drove the country to unbearable difficulties but cut it off from global development. The political decision to get rid of the foreign debt deprived our enterprises of advanced technology and resulted in uncompetitive products.

Finally, to make up for the increasing production costs of an inefficient economy and an outmoded technology dependent upon foreign markets, the State, the master of prices, made up for it through a dramatically lower standard of living for the workers. In short, the 80's were especially catastrophic for both the Romanian economy and its people, who were forced to live in hardship inconsistent with the country's degree of civilization and its ever-growing cultural level.

False statistics hid a disaster which seemed completely ignored at the top, since barely one month before the Revolution, at the 14 Romanian Communist Party Congress, Nicolae Ceaucescu was still speaking of "our economy's fiery development," while at the same time it was suffering from a general paralysis. The figures that we discovered after the Revolution surpassed our worst fears: As a whole, the results for 1989 were 5.8% worse than for 1980. During this same period, losses were 177 billion leu (during the time), without any prospect for recovery. But the most pronounced imbalances concerned industry, "the pampered child" of the socialist economy. While production and productivity decreased an average of 3 to 5% each year, manufacturing costs were increasing from 10 to 13%, so that the net product for 1000 fixed leu was only 62% of that reached in 1980.

Agriculture was not any better either and the exceptional harvests announced each year were hiding a disaster of the same magnitude.

In short, for the entire economy, the greatest problem was not a decline in production but rather the systematic falsification of reality, which was giving incredible figures for even failing projects. The Revolution inherited a Romania whose economy was in free fall. We had to assume the management of a catastrophic situation which could only get worse because of the inevitable destructurization process needed for the transition toward a market economy. During several years, the economic decline has continued, but everything leads us to believe that we have reached the end of the tunnel and that 1994 will signal the start of the recovery, the end of a difficult course which has diverted us from the chosen objectives, convinced from the very beginning that we can only pick the fruits of our labors after several years of sacrifice, perseverance and committment.

In Restrospect, What Would We Change?

When late at night I left the meetings of the Provisional Council for National Unity – where the various points of view concerning the best way to speed-up the development of Romanian society were discussed, I sometimes asked myself how long it would take us to be

able to make a precise, dispassionate and objective judgement of the period that had just ended. Through the high
price of struggle and sacrifice, we have achieved quite a
few good things during this time and it would have been
difficult to currently be without. The overthrow of a reviled system does not imply the systematic destruction of
what had been constructed in the practical domain, no
more than the indiscerning condemnation of people who
participated in the collective effort, especially knowing
that under the totalitarian regime, we had paid an exorbi-
tant price for each success and to dismiss them would be
lacking respect for those who had sacrificed to advance
Romanian society under the given conditions. Under different political regimes, swept away one by one by
History, the people accumulate a heritage and it would be
nonsense to destroy it at each stage to restart from
scratch. If "real socialism" truly disappointed us and its
outcome is "overally negative," it would still be ridiculous
to believe that during such a long stretch of time nothing
had been done, that nothing was gained by the national
culture, that there was nothing to preserve.

Even if it is still difficult to look peacefully at the forty
years of communism and to make a calm assessment of
what they brought, despite everything, to Romania, I must
recognize how the economic fabric of Romania has
changed since the war, and in a good way.

Right before World War II, at the time when part of the
population was leading a comfortable Western lifestyle in
Bucharest, then having the reputation of a "little Paris," this
Romania, whose cultivated elite and avant-gardists had
such a strong presence abroad, was nonetheless an agricul-

tural nation; 80% of the population lived in the country, with a very modest industry controlled by foreign capital. This is just an observation, and I will make it again today, by attributing it to a historic development which deprived our country of what Fernand Braudel considers as the sine qua non of the development of societies on the brink of modern times: "its calm, or relatively calm, social waters allow accumulation to take place which directs and maintains the flow, so that, with the monetary economy helping it, capitalism can finally emerge." At the time when Western Europe was moving toward a market economy and a social order that gave it its prosperity today, the different state components of modern Romania were separated under foreign occupation and exploitation (the Ottoman Empire, Russia, Austro-Hungarian Empire), incessant wars and continual trouble. If the Romanians occupied their land since ancient times, the first lasting union (after a short-lived attempt at the end of the 16 century) was in 1859; Romania became an independant and sovereign State in 1877 and it did not recover the whole of its territory until 1918.

The twenty years between the two wars were also not particularly peaceful. If Romania had seen more favorable times, nevertheless its conditions did not allow it to make up for the backwardness accumulated during the centuries during which the West had achieved its extraordinary economic leap, the accumulation of capital being done without any regard for democracy, the rights of individuals and populations – especially colonized populations – and without concern for social justice.

The most spectacular gain for Romania was certainly cultural. This country which had a 30% illiteracy rate at the end of the war no longer has any. The length of free and obligatory education went from four to ten years and our universities turned out a large stratum of intellectuals, especially a technical intelligentsia, comparable on all points to that which is found in developed countries.

The State system we had just abandoned offered, in the cultural domain, a certain number of advantages which represent for us today another type of social gain and that it would both be difficult and irresponsible to sell off cheaply. All of this was done, it's true, within the confines of a totalitarian system.

Reality demands a preliminary conclusion: it is imperative to relieve the State of several responsibilities which were imposed upon it by communist ideology, and especially to allow it to free itself of the exclusive ownership of the means of production – through which it secured a function of control to direct not only the entire economy, but also people's conscience. The State can be no more than a regulator which leaves the door open to private initiative, supported by domestic or foreign capital. It can only encourage and apply economic initiatives – this is its duty – without taking the place of economic agents, which within the framework of a market economy, must function independently. The State must also facilitate and promote adequate levers, assure the social protection of citizens and the defense of the national interest.

It is, clearly, the beginning of a road, but we have hardly begun to take the first steps, at the same time that structural reform changes are bringing about painful effects on the social level. Unfortunately, I am convinced that it is not just the right but the only path.

Transitional Dilemnas

S o now what? A troubling question for those that have taken the time to ask it.

Where do we go from here? What do we do? Towards which horizon do we direct societies just having escaped from a communist party dictatorship and Soviet domination? Obviously, towards a democratic and pluralistic government, towards a Constitutional State and a market economy by attempting to construct a free and open society worthy, in time, of European integration. If, at the time, no one challenged these movingly demanded objectives, few were the analysts and politicians who foresaw the difficulties of the road which lay ahead.

From the first days, we were under an avalanche of priorities and emergencies we had to resolve. By going about it in a completely different way with a multitude of practical questions we were able to establish what the reform projects were lacking. Western societies were constructed from models which had taken a long time to mature, continually fine-tuned by political and social thought. This was not the case for us; we had to build day by day a completely radical transformation for the entire country. We were lacking a doctrine, a potential model and the theoretical points of reference capable of guiding us. Did we have even the slightest chance, under these circumstances, to escape amateurism, uneducated decisions, errors and the pitfalls of an unknown path?

The problems of the transition did not take long to appear. How do we demolish a system solidified over forty-five years without depriving society of an institutional shelter?

How do we combine the liberties acquired with the need to reestablish public order and the State's authority? How do we abolish the centralized economy when the market economy was still not in place? Distressing questions to which we, nevertheless, had to respond, and quickly, because, in any case, society had cast off and it was dangerous to let it go adrift.

The domestic pressure to obtain rapid changes was oppressive, and on the international scene, events were taking place at an equally astounding speed. To consolidate the democratic development and to give it consistency, we had to immediately begin another revolution: an economic revolution.

At first, groups eager for electoral success at any price disturbed public opinion with Utopian and unrealistic promises which did not take into account practical restaints. This parade of radicalism hung on for a long time in Romania. Lack of experience, the inherent hesitation on an unknown journey, the political and social turmoil of the two years following the Revolution, the authority crisis of the new institutions destined to replace those which had disintegrated, the strikes, the pressure of the circumstances – everything converged to hinder the reform strategy we had designed.

The Need for a Transition Strategy

A ware of the complexity of the road that lay ahead to replace an authoritarian and extremely centralized economy with a market economy, concerned with social questions, starting in December 1989, a few days after the

Revolution, the Council of the National Salavation Front decided to create a National Institute for Economic Research likely to take charge of establishing a reform strategy. It began working in the first days of 1990, under the direction of Mr. Tudorel Postolache, also Vice-Prime Minister. In April, we had at our disposal a "Strategic Blueprin for transition to a Market Economy," whose synthesis we published in May.

Convinced of the absolute necessity of a long term vision – a subject which was at the center of my 1990 and 1992 electoral campaigns – I, myself, participated in certain of this Institute's meetings. The diversity of the points of view was wide and everyone vigorously defended them with appealing arguments. Debates of a great intellectual quality and lacking a partisan spirit allowed for the gradual establishment of a coherent economic strategy based on scientific arguments. In the difficult conditions of the transition, the economy should be a common ground for consensus. At a moment when the different political winds were confronting each other with extreme violence, not hesitating to stir up the streets to support them in often doubtful battles, I was greatly comforted by the studious and responsible climate of this Institute, whose researchers came from diverse political backgrounds, sometimes polar opposites, and who backed each other up in the name of the national interest.

I was also delighted to observe that in this field, scientists had known how to overcome the dicatorship's difficulties and bans to keep themselves up to date on advances elsewhere, to inquire and think. Because of this, immediately after the Revolution, a series of hypotheses and ingenious economic solutions appeared which has benefited us from the beginning. That also explains the speed with which the Institute was able to draw up the "Strategic Blueprint for transition to a Market Economy."

This "Blueprint" was at the same time a check-up of the Romanian economy. It took stock of the deadlocks inherited from the centralized economy, and proposed a reform program of the macro- and micro-structures of industry, agriculture, commerce and tertiary sector, replacing its old economic and financial mechanisms with others geared for a market economy. The text also recommended a staggered privatization, liberalizing prices, of foreign commerce, the convertibility of national currency, etc.

In a few important areas (liberalizing prices, the convertibility of currency, privatization of State enterprises), we studied several variations and finally decided on the one which seemed strategically appropriate with the best chances of being accepted by the people, aware that this was an indispensable condition: no economic reform could succeed without the necessary social support.

This "blueprint" guided us in the creation of the government's operational programs. Unfortunately, for varied and complex reasons, things did not turn out in the best way. Mircea Ciumara, scientific secretary of the National Institute of Economic Research and one of the important oppostion figures, was correct in saying that, after a few months, the minister in charge of economic reform had strayed away from the program inspired by the "blueprint" approved by all parliamentary groups on June 28, 1990. This provoked political tensions and, unfortunate, social unrest. Thus, the liberalization of prices should have been better prepared with estimation and expert appraisals which would have evaluated the social consequences of such a measure and spared us dangerous turmoil.

Where Did We Begin?

Experience proves that economic system reform is a great deal more difficult than that of the political system. Its inertia prevents us from making it quickly develop, and any structural change depends on the degree of social tolerance.

The Romanian economy should be reformed from top to bottom, which would involve a complete renewal of the legislative system, institutions, mechanisms, and financial and economic levers and especially a changing of mentalities – which, resistant to administrative interventions, can single-handedly sink any innovative process, hindering it by various and contradictory motivations, through various interests and by uncontrollable and unsuspected subjective processes. Ideally, an economic reform should be preceded by reforming ways of thinking, but this is not always possible.

In addition, the Revolution had brought everyone to a frenzy which expressed itself through radical and excessive behavior. It gave everyone's deeds an often pernicious haste and desperation. The ease with which we could propose them "methods," "techniques" and "therapies" capable of bringing us the dreamed prosperity made many believe that the transition was a matter of days, if not hours; that it was a simple bookkeeping operation, surgical at worst, that could be carried out right away, before even having a sure diagnosis, without any pre-operation preparation.

Where do we start?

Above all we needed to give back autonomy to the various industries to enable them to live freely, according to their own economic logic, released from the State's burdensome protection. Even before we had the time to create a strategy and rules of this particulary complex process, it had already started spontaneously, during the Revolution. The chaotic liquidation, from one day to the next, of the State Planning Committee and institutions in charge of coordinating the economic processes, as well as the unthinking abolition of specific mechanisms of the centralized economy before those of the market economy still had a chance to replace them, had a formidable destructive effect. Some people were convinced that all which we had inherited from the previous regime was rotten and claimed that our only chance was to make a clean sweep and to start all over from scratch. Our industry was "a heap of scrap metal," then what good would it do to persist in working and making machines operate which it was better to throw it in the garbage? People were abandoning work sites and equipment was consequently disappearing.

On the other hand, experienced people with certain skills, who would have been able to more or less maintain a balance and positively channel the overflowing energy during the months which followed the Revolution, were thrown out with the accused, most often gratuitously for complicity with the former regime, which had simply allowed them to practice their know-how. If this movement allowed us to get rid of a certain number of individuals who under the former regime had obtained responsibilities which neither their professional abilities nor their moral qualities entitled them to, dilettantes and erratic people, also, took advantage of this to give themselves positions for which they did not have the least qualification. The consequences for the national economy were disastrous.

Agriculture was suffering from its own earthquake.

Just after the Revolution, the farmers seemed satisfied to have recovered the fields they were working in the collective farms when the rural world started to erupt into turmoil. Commendable, though it could have been improved, Law 18 re-established the right to own land. At the same time, it was a concession which didn't benefite the farmers, the agricultural production, or the people's food supply. Forced in the past to form collective farms which, far from being free associations, represented a way for the State to better exploit them, farmers were now the first to ask for the immediate abolition of any form of collective property, which was done through an act perhaps not entirely unselfish and, certainly, hasty. If the collective farms were not very profitable in certain regions where the landscape did not lend itself to such use, others used intensive and modern agriculture and benefited from irrigation systems (3 million hectares) and State investments for soil clean-up which obtained excellent results and got rich, disposing of considerable means, abundant livestock and securing a high income for its members.

Law 18 grants the land back to its former owners, of which, unfortunately, today there often only remains the inheritors, especially city dwellers who have never worked in them and who do not have the least intention to do so. This led to an excessive parcelling of farms. As we could expect from it, confusion – which some people fueled, not always innocently – between the right to own land, the property size and managing the farm prevented the quick recovery of Romanian agriculture and resulted in a decline in production.

The new government could have re-established the right to own property without disbanding healthy agricultural production units. The examples of Hungary, the former Czechoslovakia, and even the ex-East Germany are con- clusive on this. Likewise, some of our cooperatives reorga- nized themselves into commercial businesses selling shares, others into landowners' associations which gave encouraging results. Better still, ingenious systems for the distribution of shares enabled members to differentiate ac- cording to the number of years that they had worked on the association's lands, which assured a more equitable distribution of income. It is always easy to dismantle and a great deal more difficult to reconstruct or to create some- thing new.

The State institutions were also undergoing a deep au- thority crisis. No one obeyed anyone else any more. In ad- dition, certain people conveyed the preposterous idea of a general guilt which they could atone for only through a kind of social and political purification on a national scale, everyone forced to take on the sins of some, everyone brought to discover imaginary faults, an entire people locked in a kind of collective suffering.

Well, thanks to the radically dramatic nature of our Revolution, Romania has benefited from a surge of sympathy and solidarity coming from beyond its borders. Nevertheless, I believe that very large segments of the population started to wrongly hope that we could excuse ourselves from our own work and from our own sacrifices, the West having the means to straighten out our economy. Indeed, foreign aid has been of great help to us, especially moral, but, clearly, it cannot replace the work put in by the entire country.

In short, everyone was looking for something, but without exactly knowing what.

The pressure of the circumstances was intense, and in a certain way, explainable. An explosion as violent as the Romanian Revolution does not exhaust all its energy with one blow, and before going back to normal, society is still shaken by sudden and unexpected aftershocks. A demand brings on another and were inevitably aimed at a power that some people were convinced (according to plans inherited from the old regime) that it could do anything and had the means to resolve any problem by opening its wallet.

It is also very true that to indicate the direction of its economic and social choices, the government had taken a series of measures favoring a certain class of citizen as early as December 1989, enthusiastic but sometimes hasty measures, certainly necessary but which aggravated the state of the national economy.

To relieve a population which had faced enormous difficulties over the years, forced to live in unacceptable conditions of food and energy shortages, deprived of food, warmth, electricity, etc., the government, in spite of limited resources, made considerable efforts to improve daily life. It also decided to return to wage-earners the social funds held back the last few years to make up the social capital of State enterprises (around 30 billion leu in 1990). It allocated funds to increase low salaries and better compensate difficult work, help farmers, increase the number of retired people (doubled through the reduction of the retirement age) – measures politically and socially indispensable but economically risky. In the post-Revolutionary climate, it was impossible to resist these social pressures which aimed to restore basic rights which the former regime had made a mockery of.

For lack of other means, in 1990 we spent nearly all of our investment funds (297 of the 300 billion leu) to improve living conditions. This was not a way to corrupt the voters, as some people reproach us for; they had already voted. It was a political choice to protect a fledgling democracy, of which no one was the sole beneficiary. This policy, which was already moving toward a reform freeing the State from its role as the economic investor, could only aggravate, although in a barely significant way, the decline of industrial production which we no longer had the means to support. Certain domains were abandoned outright, including the construction of State housing, the energy infrastructures, and hydrotechnic development.

Good or bad, these emergency measures were not meant to bring about definitive solutions but to give us time to establish a correct diagnosis and to elaborate a coherent reform strategy equipped with several plans of implementation in order to have potential well thought out, responses at hand, capable of helping us face the different economic circumstances of a developing society, and to also keep our possibilities in mind.

Nevertheless, it was a pioneering period, because, if these measures did not manage to define reform in its entirety, they at least allowed us to head in that direction.

So Where Are The Reforms?

O nce again, commentators did not restrain themselves from giving, in this domain just as in others, analyses cleverly expressing their political opinions. If "the Revolution did not happen" or if it was really nothing but a "production," a "palace revolution," naturally reform itself "never took place," or, at best, it was "slowed down." If the Revolution was "confiscated" and "diverted," reform could only be a more or less clever way to mask the "restoration." What restoration? The one of the "neo and crypto-communists," of course.

Political folklore continues to thrive without taking into account other fringes of public opinion which accuse the State and the Government of wanting to reform too much too fast, or reforming indiscriminately and paying too high a social price considering our mind states.

A legitimate question: Where are the reforms?

I do not think it is necessary to return to the very first measures, which were just transitory. The enthusiasm of the time explains their incoherence and feverishness: decentralization, liberalization of domestic and foreign commerce, free pricing, reform of the banking system and so on. Very quickly we produced a "Strategic Blueprint for Reform," which was very useful in this uncertain period, yet we were overcome by the events, which were raising unexpected questions we needed to immediately answer with practical responses.

The solutions which enabled us to overcome the political crisis did not manage to resolve the economic one, and the stability that we succeeded in maintaining is just a prerequisite for the deep structural changes which demand more time and effort on everyone's part. The difficulties inherent in the transition set off another crisis and provoked deadlock of another kind, all the more dangerous for our recovery and our integration into the European and world economic lifelines. We were at the crossroads of several crises, stuck in a very unenviable position.

Our difficulties today have at least three causes: the destructurization of the centralized State economy, the reconversion of an industry dependent on energy, raw materials and foreign markets, and finally, a mismanaged agriculture. All this in unfavorable general economic circumstances, in a context of a global and European economy itself shaken by a deep and lasting crisis. Romania also had the misfortune to inherit important economic relations with either war-ravaged countries (Iraq, Kuwait, ex-Yugoslavia), or with countries undergoing changes themselves (Russia, Ukraine, and all former Soviet block countries). This situation deprived us of energy supplies and raw materials as well as foreign markets – which shrank if not disappeared altogether. This aggravated our decline in industrial production with predictable consequences: deterioration of the foreign trade balance, lowered value of our resources, devaluation of the national currency, unemployment and inflation. The reforms began with one of its principal plans levers being privatization, which refers to big as well as small enterprises. Concerning small enterprises, there presently exist around 500,000 private units formed, especially around the beginning of 1993, which employ approximately 2 million people, which is about as many people as State-owned enterprises. This means that the private sector already represents a dynamic factor in the national economy.

If small and medium-size privatization is headed down the right road, that of the giant enterprises has only just begun, and for a very good reason. One law established the way of privatizing the 6000 State-run enterprises, which became autonomous commercial businesses. Until today, the State has only succeeded in privatizing 450 small and medium-sized enterprises.

A straight forward analysis of the situtation leads me to believe that the recovery of the Romanian economy can only come about with the support of foreign capital, and in my discussions with industrialists and financial analysts from prestigious companies, I established that investors were beginning to have an interest in our country.

Moreover, we succeeded in halting the decline in agricultural production. It is obviously difficult to give a recently privatized agricultural system the means it requires for recovery, but it is in everyone's best interest. The State did not intervene through measures which would risk upsetting a farming class already mistrustful due to past brutalities. At the same time, if certain imperfections in the basic law and abuses in its implementation sometimes created tensions in the farming world, it is out of the question to allow the deliberately maintained confusion to self-perpetuate concerning the differences between property rights, the size of the property and the type of farming done on the land – three totally distinct notions. The belief that excessive division of the land by the appearance of several thousand small farmers lacking the technical and financial means is a way to succeed in profitable farming in fact only leads to a decline in production. This does not mean we should call property rights into question. Even less when we observe that by accepting 50 hectare properties, as some of today's five million land-owners are asking for, there would only be 200,000 of them left in the short-term. What would become of the others? A good half live in town, but the other half is too profoundly attached to the land; to lose it would be traumatic for them. Do we want to make them employees on large farms, the new agricultural proletariat, and the rural unemployed? Where could they go since industry, itself in the middle of reconstruction, no longer needs a labor force? I am passing over the fact that those who are demanding the right to recover the large properties are also demanding to have the mountains, all of the forests, the subsoil, the waterways, everything. Would we go back fifty, one hundred, five hundred years, before the land reforms of the 19th century which aimed to put an end to the misery that the Romanian farming class was suffering? It is not only unrealistic, because it goes against the flow of history, but also immoral. How could we also ignore the development of the past fifty years and the buildings constructed sometimes on the old properties: factories, roads, hydoelectric and hydrotechnical installations? How do you forget that the land register has been deeply changed? Do we want to destroy everything so that the properties resemble what they were before the war? And then to award landowners from the past the properties belonging to others who have toiled in them, who have paid for them and who have enjoyed them for such a long time? Where is the justice in this?

Obviously, the various agricultural interests are immense. The intensity with which some people maintain harmful tensions without even being based in the rural world is not likely to bring the necessary confidence and serenity for the long awaited recovery. Yet my hope continues that good sense will prevail, and that everyone will agree that we cannot repair past wrongs by wronging others whose only fault was entering into the world later and to have living in a system now collapsed. That said, other objective criteria exists to appraise the degree of the economic reform's implementation. I believe I can honestly assert that in only four years, and in spite of the fact that no one had market economy experience, we have still travelled a considerable distance on this journey.

In spite of the diversity of points of view, which, nevertheless, was a great help in clarifying our own ideas, we ended up working out a reform strategy to guide us in the transition toward a market economy. A great number of the legislative and executive measures already mark the road followed in this journey. Due to the nature of the presidency, I was perhaps the first to notice that we had made mistakes, some inevitable, others less so, which, however, at no moment called into question the reform itself. To appreciate what was done by avoiding extreme positions, we have to take into account the general context and realize that, under the circumstances, it was difficult to do better. The various governments did only what was reasonable in the difficult conditions where they had to act, acquitting themselves more or less well of their task without ever losing sight of the reform's concrete objectives. It is in the interest of the entire country neither to dishearten it by letting it believe that it is still in the starting blocks nor to demobilize it by leading it to believe that it has reached the end of its sorrows.

The reform passes through stages which are determined by the degree of political stability and the consolidation of the Constitutional State, by taking into account the real situation of an already suffering economy whose transition toward a market economy still aggravates its decline. The reform should first of all put an end to the economy's degradation. It was all the more laborious since the transition's difficulties, painfully felt by the entire people, were originally a number of social reactions that the government did not always know how to resolve in the best way, sometimes even having provoked them with incoherent or poorly prepared measures – which also had political repercussions capable of shaking the climate of stability absolutely necessary to make the proposed reforms succeed.

Economic reform clearly demands a subtle and difficult-to-achieve balance between the different necessary measures and what a society is able to withstand. Not taking this into account is dangerous and even risks challenging the reform itself, different groups of citizens rejecting it because they are in temporary difficulties. The practices of Central and Eastern European countries, which, one way or another, are following the same path as Romania, prove that progress never goes in a straight line. What is important is to stay the course while at the same time following the curves imposed by the circumstances. Romania can congratulate itself for having known how to preserve political stability and for having followed a general economic direction whose price we had to pay for with the hope that the benefits would not be long in coming.

I was and still am convinced that in order to face the sometimes unpredictable and always dangerous situations caused by reform, the government, whatever its form or political orientation, must rely on all of the political forces which, despite differences and sensibilities, share the same interest of strengthening democracy and establishing a market economy. This puts us in the position to have a rapid pace of development, and finally, a standard of living comparable to that of European countries to whom we feel linked through our traditions, our history, our culture and our civilization.

The Course of Reform
and Specific Pressures

Re-structurization and privatization imply effort and sacrifice, doubt and disillusionment, waiting and uncertainty which traumatize the social fabric, something which I must always keep in mind. Price increases, inflation, unstable employment, difficulties in meeting the everyday needs of life are a reality and, even more painful, some particular groups such as retired people, students, large families and the unemployed are particularly suffering from the transtition's harmful effects.

I, nevertheless, consider that the gloomy and catastrophic image that some give the situation is dangerous in so far as it deliberately ignores the ongoing changes and road travelled to overcome the crisis; they lead us to believe that we are at the edge of chasm and without any chance of overcoming the challenges that we are facing.

Without being spectacular, the results which we have already obtained constitute the promise of an impending growth and prove that the reform has not been ineffective. Overstating (especially for political reasons) the economic difficulties which we must face provokes natural reactions which push a part of the people toward excessive and pernicious attitudes, capable of endangering not only the reform itself but also the State's balance and stability. This is in a European context where it would be irresponsible to not note the resurgence of nationalism, sometimes violent inter-ethnic confrontations, the rise of extremism and the proliferation of organizations and movements claiming allegiance to them. It is my duty to give a few details about this.

First appearing in 1990, our political, ethnic and even religious extremism is explained above all by a precarious economic situation which leads some to believe that the exclusion of others can protect them from a misery whose causes are found elsewhere. Fueled by diverse and not always commendable interests, this extremism which opposes even on the political scene diverse ethnic and social groups, developed at a moment when the still fragile State institutions did not have sufficient authority to suppress it. Some irredentists and jingoists took advantage of them to inflame spirits and provoke through statements offensive to the Romanian people, understandable but nevertheless regretable reactions.

At the extreme right, the most troubling movements affiliated themselves with the fascist ideology of pre-war Romanian legionnaires. Supported by a fringe of emigration which put propaganda at its disposal, the legionnaire movement makes assiduous recruitment efforts and to make its "Iron Guard" official. It also tried to revise history and whitewash the legionnaire movement whose responsibility in the tragic events of 1930-40 are clearly established and undeniable. Exploiting the material difficulties of some as well as the irresponsible provocations of a few extremist circles belonging to ethnic minorities, the legionnaires were looking for support among young people, misfits and nationalists. Their activity doubtlessly takes advantage of the State institutions' lack of firmness, which worried more about respecting the recently recovered individual liberties and hesitated to make allowances and to restrict them for those who abuse them[1].

Left-wing extremism, on the other hand, does not seem to constitute a danger. We can, nevertheless, reproach certain individuals for a demagogic discourse capable of reinforcing the mistrust of a part of the people toward the Constitutional State and provoking fanatic individual reactions likely to throw the State off balance and unleashing reactions wiser to avoid.

I am convinced that the appeal of extremists comes from their ability to manipulate vague concepts and to practice a demagoguery which rejects clear ideas as well as the pre-

---

1. My position concerning the publication and distribution of "Mein Kampf" and a certain number of legionnaire texts has aroused controversy. I continue to believe that the "freedom of information" does not justify the publication of this type of work.

cise evaluation of political, economic and social consequences at the national level. The best way of fighting them
is to appeal to the people's intelligence, by asking them to
note the lack of realism in the proposed solutions and to
look at the experience of History, which provides so many
tragic examples of situations which people succumbed to
when taken in by such dangerous ideologies.

I ask for the same firmness for certain political demonstrations which try to resolve in the streets the battle of ideas
and opinions natural in a democracy, and to have solutions
accepted by force and disorder which did not win at the
ballot box. I am trying to make Romanian society see that
anarchy does not serve the national interest and the best
way to move forward is to reinforce the Constitutional
State, which guarantees the liberty of all and the respect of
one another. Indeed, I am not including social movements
which sometimes make their claims known through street
demonstrations with those who abuse it to provoke trouble
and incite disturbances with the goal of maintaining a climate of insecurity. The later hope to damage the democratic institutions and to protest the choices freely expressed
by the majority of voters, defying constitutional rules and
the interests of an entire people anxious for serenity and
social peace after all the ordeals they have undergone.

As a supporter of national reconciliation (I am absolutely
convinced of the need for it and I have called for it every
time I had the chance) I cannot accept a laissez-faire attitude whose dangers I see every day just by looking at what
is happening in our neighboring countries. I condemn with
the same firmness the political and social voluntarism
which wants to impose measures without taking into ac-

count public opinion, thus opening the door to arbitrariness and constitutes the denial of democracy. Extremist movements would conjure up all the ghosts whose ravages we have learned firsthand: jingoism, xenophobia, nationalism, antisemitism, irredentism. Without exceeding my prerogative as Chief of State, I ask the Republic's institutions and those in charge to have the constitutional measures be respected and to be uncompromising toward extremists of all stripes who openly deride them.

It is also necessary to be vigilant toward certain forms of political and social nostalgia which exerts a double pressure on people's minds. On the one hand, those who have lost privileges through the disappearance of the centralized and interventionist system take advantage of the current difficulties to paint the abolished regime in a good light and to evoke the possibility of a return to a State economy which led us to a catastrophe whose magnitude we are still assessing today. On the other hand, those who claim that "nothing has been done" and that under the cover of a hypothetical economic reform, we are in fact witnessing a "restoration," want to speed up the progress to an pace unbearable for the entire people, which risks calling everything into question by pushing the people toward attitudes of unbending refusal.

I want to affirm to everyone that the economic reform can neither be stopped nor avoided. It is an inescapable historic process desired by the entire people, who would know how to impose it by force if conservative activists tried to derail it, who would also know how to curb it if the required sacrifices and efforts surpassed the threshold of tolerance permissible on the social plan. In addition, a return to where we started would require the same ordeals in the opposite direction, which would be an unimaginable national catastrophe. Anyway, we do not need an exceptional political insight to understand that in today's national and international scene, an interventionist-style economy is no longer conceivable. With whom and with what means could such an economy connect, through what mechanisms could it integrate itself within the global economy since this system has disintegrated everywhere, victim of an inefficiency which no one doubts any more?

Nostalgia of a more distant past, that of the period between the two wars, is no less unrealistic. It would aim to rebuild according to the principle of "restitutio in integrium" a world long since disappared, as if we could go back in time fifty years, ignoring what has since happenned in Romania and in the world[1]. It would have to pretend to forget that regardless of the means used and the imposed suffering, Romanian society has undergone profound structural changes these last fifty years. During this period people's attitudes have greatly evolved and new generations naturally have points of view different than those of half a century ago.

I find it timely to point out the social after-effects of a parasitic mentality, inherited from decades of bureaucratic communism. A certain number of individuals had it easy, protected by a cocoon that must not be disturbed and which they were still trying to maintain, refusing on principle any effort and any social change likely to call into question their professional and personal comfort. We must add to them a fringe of profiteers who know how to exploit the

---

1. This movement's political slogan is "the Monarchy will save Romania," and its dream is to restore the State structures from prior to the war.

problems of this transition period, the legislative cracks and the fragility of the institutions to get rich through practices which, especially at the State level, slow down the reform. Corruption, a kind of heavy tax unfairly paid by honest citizens, tax evasion and even a certain kind of mercenariness, moral degradation and contempt for the work ethic, underestimating the State's patrimony at the moment of privatizations and underestimating the national interest in international commercial transactions have taken alarming proportions detrimental not only to the idea of reform, which seems to wrongly benefit swindlers and crooks, but also to the balances of the entire society, destabilized by the fraudulent practices of a few. I do not believe that I am exceeding my powers by asking the State institutions to be more vigilant and severe toward those who are taking advantage of our difficulties to fish in troubled waters with no regard for the law. We need to immediately enact a civil service statute and a rapid ratification of provisions concerning the obligation of those taking on positions to make their patrimony known at the time they enter office to the moment that they leave it.

Obviously, I'm counting on the self-regulating mechanisms of the market economy to get rid of, with the support of the judicial system and financial controls, the pains that Romaian society is suffering today: corruption, fraud, speculation, unfair competition, abuse, and breach of trust. The natural and respectable ambition to enrich oneself must be based on work, investment risks, and the competence and courage of entrepreneurs who respect the law. All of these pressures and nostalgia, this dubious behavior and these vicious habits obey their own logic which ends

up being some political expression always related to reform, a sort of counter-current, which far from clarifying
matters, makes the waters muddy and causes threatening
waves. Nostalgic demagoguery of all kinds exists, another
of negation at all costs, and some are starting to practice
these with true savoir-faire. But for someone taking an
honest and objective and realistic look, there is no doubt –
reform is already on its way and it is not taking us to a recent or distant past, but toward the future.

Where We Are Now
and What Must Still Be Accomplished

I think the words that best define Romania today are
revolution and reform, two poles between which all of
the processes destined to give Romania a new, modern,
European image are developing.
Revolution because this social and political upheaval left
its mark on Romania in 1989 and still continues to affect its
evolution.
Reform because Romania is on its way to becoming a
Constitutional State and creating a market economy where
society can bloom.
Revolution and reform make up two sides of the same coin
which together are transforming Romania from top to bottom into a modern country. Reform and revolution are
casting light on and nourishing one another in this transition period which is leading Romanian society from revolution to evolution.

In fact, the turmoil which has shaken Romanian society in the two years following the December 1989 Revolution has prevented politicians from starting deep, coherent, structural changes. We had to wait for the new Constitution to be drawn up, for several political winds to appear – social-democrats, christian-democrats, liberals-, and for legitimate local, legislative and presidential elections. We also had to wait for the Constitutional State and its institutions to be solid enough for the new powers to put the radical measures into action which were destined to transform the very basis society.

However, the economy put up resistance which was infinitely more difficult to conquer. The past heritage was weighty, and this is where the majority of structures to demolish or reconvert existed, without even counting that here is where the most pernicious form of selfishness appears. Is it necessary to add that the social dimension of reform directly depended on economic results which had to ensure a better standard of living and adequate social protection, enough to discourage nostalgia for the old system and to dissipate doubts concerning the direction and the need for reform?

1993 was the most difficult. Economic decline reached a critical point with grave social consequences: unemployment and inflation. This was also the year when the government had the courage to enact several painful but necessary measures in order for the reform to succeed, including the abolition of subsidies for basic products and services and the introduction of the VAT tax. At the same time, without the foreign financial support needed for such an important operation and despite a negative commercial

balance, the government, convinced of the need to stabilize the national currency, allowed foreign exchange rates
to be freely established, the official rate corresponding to
demand.

Our efforts were rewarded: this same year, economic decline stopped and we recorded a very slight increase in
foreign trade. After two years of drought, the production of
grain was sufficient enough to allow us to decrease our imports, which will also benefit our balance of payments.

1994 will be decisive in so far as we will succeed in stabilizing the currency, reducing inflation and interest rates, increasing production and exports. Also decisive is that conditions are right to start privatizing large enterprises and
to attract the foreign capital needed to reconstruct and
modernize several vital industrial sectors and also the in-
frastructure (roads, railroads, telecommunications, energy
and hydrotechnology). The State can then distribute the
funds necessary for a more coherent social assistance program, especially favoring certain underprivileged groups.
This would also have a decisive impact on the job market
by reducing unemployment with the creation of new jobs,
especially for young people, and by stimulating the reconversion of the workforce.

Moreover, the reform must be more far-reaching, have an
economic efficiency and rationality with a long term vision. New regulations should clarify responsibilities in the
management of State enterprises which we can no longer
manage without taking into account the good or bad
recorded results. The reform can only succeed if it goes
on to the level of productive units. These should be supported to reform by themselves, according to their own

ability to adapt themselves to a market economy. We have reached a point where the reform itself must be de-centralized.

This assumes a few priorities: the expansion of the private sector, the substantial restructuring of industry, the reorganization of the financial and banking system, the revival of agriculture, the reduction of inflation and the strengthening of the national currency to stimulate foreign capital investments, cooperation and international exchanges, all while protecting the national economy, especially our industries capable of developing an overseas competitiveness.

In turn, the State must accelerate legislative activity and obtain a better coordination of the organizations in charge of implementing the reform, which assumes a common action of all the country's political forces, unions, government institutions, economic mediums and production units.

Regarding the general development of the private sector's economic activity, I see three priorities. The first and most important one relates to the national strategy that we must develop. It should define a long-term perspective and our objective for the national economy, not only in keeping with reality – today's, our nation's, and developed countries'(among these, the European Community which one day we hope to join), but by also taking the future into account. Shaken by a deep, structural crisis, the developed countries will not pull through without substantial changes, which will bring upheavals to the entire global economy. We have to take this into account to prepare our country to what this new world economic order will be and in a way, take advantage of the reform we are implementing to avoid the tunnel that developed countries are crossing and meet them instead at the exit which we would have reached through another route. Technological advances, especially in computers, have changed the face of Western economies, which no longer manage to have full employment. We should restructure our economy by taking into account the new realities appearing in the world. A year ago, I had very useful discussions about this at the Crans-Montana World Economic Forum, in Switzerland: worried about the difficulties of the transition, the Eastern countries' representatives were expecting aid and promises of cooperation on the part of the West. They heard that even the Western countries are not finding solutions to the problems facing them. We told them that the only chance of pulling through was to do it together. The West will not be able to face its problems if it remains mired in a protectionist policy, if it considers cooperation with Eastern countries with the conceit of the wealthy, by taking us only for a market of its own products and by refusing to accept us as partners. The development of Central and Eastern European countries is an opportunity for Western countries as well as for ourselves.

I consider it my duty to also answer those who assert more or less openly that the development of Central and Eastern European countries constitutes a danger for the West, which has no reason to support the recovery of its potential competitors. This reasoning is false. Developed countries trade primarily among themselves – thus, 80% of Switzerland's foreign trade is done with the European Community. In fact, the developed countries have a diversified economy, the division of labor is infinitely more precise and the products necessary for their national markets are found primarily in countries having the same economic potential. According to this same logic, the economic development of Central and Eastern European countries will make interesting markets appear for developed countries and will also allow them to find the products they need in these countries. The broadening of the developing countries' markets can only help everyone, bringing each country's economy an additional dynamic force.

The question is to know how we can find our place in the global and European economy. In developed countries new activities will inevitably appear, which will require more and more intellectual creativity. Talent will develop in the fields of art, culture and leisure activities. We are headed toward development structures completely different than those we have known up to now. It is into this process that we must integrate. If we satisfy ourselves with catching up to the developed countries, we will still be behind, because these countries, in the meantime, will have taken a different route, according to a new dynamic. We thus need a long-term vision, corresponding to our own real possibilities but in keeping with the demands of out time, the end of the century. This would be the first decisive step of the development strategy which we need to immediately define.

Another priority is the suppression of inflation, a phenomenon which is dominating our economic life and is creating enormous difficulties in our day to day life. We do not yet have a market economy with its own self-regulating mechanisms. The state-controlled administrative mechanisms which could combat and stop the price surge no longer exist and we do not want them to. We must intervene in other ways, especially by stimulating production in order to lower cost prices and to discourage speculation. While we wait, we must enact legislative measures to prevent this specultation. Generally speaking, we must also bring back the idea of social order and respect for democratic law and values.

Lastly, we must stabilize the national currency, which can only be done by balancing the scales of foreign trade. We have no foreign resources and no one will give us any gifts. In economic policy, generosity and humanitarianism do not go hand in hand. The only interest that governs economic policy is self-interest. We must find the means to satisfy both individual and social interests, national interests and those of our economic partners. We do not and never have had cash reserves. The only way for us to balance our accounts and to support national currency is to have a stable trade balance. During these last four years, we have deliberately taken on a trade deficit. In fact, after such a long period of near total interruption in our foreign dealings, the need for imported goods was so great that it would have been difficult to stop it, even if it did not always correspond to absolute necessity. At the same time, our exports saw a net reduction because of the collapse of certain markets in which we were established and the difficulty of entering others. I think it is high time to establish a sensible system of economic levers which encourages exports and discourages imports, especially in areas where we have our own production. We must make all of the necessary arrangements to better develop our production potential and to help modernize all businesses which are likely to become competitive in the global market.

We must all face the facts: until we get production back on its feet with new methods and exports become more important than imports to allow us to accumulate cash reserves, we will not have the necessary resources to invest, to modernize our businesses and infrastructures, to noticibly increase the standard of living and to give considerably more support to activities which depend on the national budget, that is, culture, education, health and defense.

Soon after the Revolution, we were aware that the transition would be difficult and I gave several warnings about it. I specifically pointed out that it was necessary to keep a balance between the economic and social components of reform to avoid jeopardizing this reform. My opinion was sometimes hastily challenged before taking the time for sensible analysis, not even mentioning the criticism of pure bad faith. Today, almost all politicians recognize the importance of the social component and ask that it be taken into consideration. The key to a natural evolution is to realistically evaluate the degree of social tolerance, to get the people on the side of the reform and to assure them effective social protection.

Dragged away at will or by force, like all of the other countries in this area full of turmoil, while on the road to development, our efforts will not be rewarded in the same way if we allow ourselves to be carried along by the general movement rather than doing everything possible to better participate in this journey and to put forward our qualities which can best serve the common cause.

What we must ask ourselves to do right now, is to give a constructive and lasting effort. A Romania which paves the way with a fierce determination to a national destiny likely to lead it to a prosperous future will not bring happiness to just one social group, nor will it be a country run by exclusion and injustice. On the contrary, the advantages will be evenly shared between the laborers and the farmers, the business owners and the intellectuals, the civil servants and the merchants. Today, the difficulties of the transition weigh on us all; it is natural that we will all benefit together from the riches our people will produce once out of this difficult period. The change in generations which is and will remain the spirit of social change will be done with dignity. We will have the satisfaction of giving the young people, who today look towards the future with uncertainty, a country which will not let them down.

While we wait, we must roll up our sleeves and get to work.

We have to show determination and courage. Sacrifices are inevitable.

Romania is at a point in its history where it finally has the chance to free itself from all of the pressures and constraints which curbed its development in the past. Finally masters of their destiny, our people must carefully maintain the fundamental balances which will allow Romania to continue on its course without encountering any accidents, keeping in mind that success depends on their efforts and their prudence and not losing sight of the final goal or falling prey to dangerous over-eagerness. In a world full of transformation, in search of new forms of collective existence, each country and each people must follow its own path. We must preserve and consolidate what we acquire, maybe modest, still inefficient, but essential for enabling us to move ahead.

Romania's Contribution to European Stability

The changes which have taken place in Europe since 1989 have modified several essential elements of Romania's geopolitical environment. For the first time, it no longer borders a super power likely to exert pressure on it's systems. Three of its five neighbors today – Ukraine, Moldova and what's left of the former Yugoslavia (Serbia and Montenegro) – have become States within the last four years.

Along with the dissolution of the Soviet Union and Yugoslavia, we also saw the divorce of the Czech and Slovak Republics and the appearance of a large number of new States: Slovenia, Croatia, the Baltic Republics, Belarus and the Caucasus Republics. At this time, ranked by its territorial and demographic size, Romania is the ninth European country. It is the third, after Ukraine and Poland, Central European partner to be united by NATO in the Northern Atlantic Cooperation Council.

The "good neighbor policy" which has for a long time been the mainstay of Romanian foreign policy is taking on new importance. In the new European context, borders no longer hinder the global goal which aims to unite all of the countries in a common effort of development and progress serving our respective civilizations. The new reality reduces the importance of distance and give us "indirect neighbors" within zones linked by common interest and cooperation and based on economic relations and shared cultures.

Though I don't want to get carried away by examining the individual relationship we have with each one of our partners, I am nevertheless anxious to say that Romanian political efforts, in often difficult circumstances, have ended up in satisfactory results. Without ever losing sight of national interests, which can create dangerous tension, we have succeeded in recognizing other countries' concerns and nearly always finding reasonable and profitable solutions for everyone. Indeed, the publication of foreign policy matters more often concerns principles and results than detailed measures which may demand the discretion and patience of waiting for the moment when historians will judge our acts in relation to developments which today are just rough outlines. I am satisfied with highlighting the tenacity with which we enacted our foreign policy on the road to openness and dialogue with our neighbors and the fact they have almost always responded to us in a positive way. If sometimes we were misunderstood or not as coherent as we would have liked to be, this has not prevented us from pursuing a good neighbor policy. We are convinced that common efforts and reciprocal initiatives will quickly smooth out the few rough edges which are transitory and not at all insurmountable.

A common language and a history and civilization as great as our own, make the brand new Republic of Moldova a special neighbor to which each one of us feels bound by blood. I have already stated my feelings concerning the odious Molotov-Ribbentrop pact which snatched this region from our national territory, after the Vienna Diktat had already taken a part of Transylvania. I believe that with calmness, wisdom and patience, the Romanian diplomacy, the Nation's leaders and politicians on all sides must take advantage of any occasion to remind the world and international institutions of some particularly painful historical realities. Nevertheless, our relationship with the Republic of Moldova must take into account the present reality and recognize its existence as the second Romanian state.

This contradicts, I must say, the historic and natural rights of a nation of people and their desire to live between the borders of the same State. I also understand this Romanian region represents a wound for all of us as it was so brutally pulled away from our national territory. I can in no way condemn the patriotic feelings of those who would like to remedy past injustices, but, as a Statesman responsible for the destiny of Romania over the long-term, I do not think it is useful or wise to overlook today's realities and I refuse to involve Romanian policy in emotional dealings which would harm the peace and stability of the entire region. This painful question must be handled with infinitely more tact and we must have the insight to wait for favorable conditions which will hopefully bring about, through a natural process, changes which would be dangerous to rush.

Romania wholly supports the consolidation of Moldova's independence and sovereignty on a domestic and international level. All the more so since, as in the Baltic republics, there are still foreign troops on this independent State's soil. Through the hazards of history, we are not just neighbors of the Republic of Moldova but also of

Russia, which maintains its renowned 14th Army near our borders.

We would like to consider ourselves neighbors with the countries linking us to the Black Sea: Turkey, Greece, Georgia, Armenia, and Azerbaijan.

Delivered from totalitarianism, Romania today intends to take advantage of its geographical position at the crossroads of the principal areas of instability in Europe to play a role in keeping the peace and helping establish new relations with the surrounding countries. Without running the risk of sounding like a narrow-minded Eurocentrist, I do believe – and this is supported by many other political analysts worldwide – that developments in Europe and the Euro-Atlantic will continue to greatly influence the world.

To make a precise estimate of Romania's geostrategic importance and role, I believe that three essential elements must be considered: the objective parameters of its position in Europe, the international and domestic perception of the country's possibility of playing a role in this turbulent region and the conditions allowing Romania's active involvement in the regional balance of power, benefitting both Romanians and the rest of the world. Clearly, our role is dynamic and in continual development, and a judicious examination must take our potential developments into consideration.

The appearance in Europe of quite a few new States which did not always succeed in resolving all of their problems in a clear way should alter some people's intoxicated ideological vision. It should also call for a political rereading of the European map – even if, with a few exceptions, one being Mr. Jirinovski who does well to remind us that in this matter one can never be too vigilant, no one seems tempted anymore to order people's lives by running a pencil over a map.

It seems logical to me to go back to the old designation of this zone, traditionally called Central Europe. It's not only a matter of Romania being half-way between the Atlantic and the Ural Mountains, but more seriously, about avoiding a mistaken and deliberate distinction which aims to stop the European borders at the Carpathian Mountains, thus not only excluding Romania and other new democracies from the European integration process, but also cutting Romania in half with the hope of creating a territory detached enough from the country that it would be easy prey for those wanting to seize it. André and Jean Sellier, authors of the "Atlas of Central European Populations" recently published by Editions Découvertes in Paris, would not contradict me; they add historical observations and civilisation facts to their atlas in order to show that this zone only became "Eastern Europe" at the moment when it was engulfed in the Soviet Union's sphere of influence.

It's easy to see that behind the concern of integrating certain regions "into the history and destiny of Central Europe," journalists, political analysts, and worst of all, some politicians are trying to hide a very trite revisionism. Encouraged by post-communist Europe's geopolitical changes, these people are nostalgic for a lost grandeur; they believe that "now everything is possible" and that we have to take advantage of this period to obtain "historic reparations" to at least partially recover the empires fallen in the ashes of World War I. They also say that the dismemberment of Yugoslavia and the separation of the

Czech Republic and Slovakia are a sign of the "definitive collapse" of the Treaty of Versailles. I would point out to them that Romania is a country united by language, demography, religion, history and tradition and that all of the regions inside its borders today belong to a common and specific civilization. On the other hand, maybe it would be useful to ponder what would become of Europe if we questioned treaties concerning the territory of certain countries like Romania or Poland?! I recall that this kind of chiseling, always with the idea of revising the treaty of Versailles, has already been practiced by Hitler and Stalin, whose "arbitration" ended up in the Ribbentrop-Molotov pact. I believe I am not mistaken in considering that one of the fundamental tasks of those in charge of European security is to discourage such initiatives and to avert the disastrous consequences which could result from them.

The way we look at Central Europe also depends on constructing a new European order. The chances for this are limited, if instead of building a Europe of the future, we tried to restore it to how it was at the beginning of the century, if not the Middle Ages – and we know the price paid for this Europe's "adventures."

Clearly, the concrete problem of a European State belonging to a particular sub-region of the continent may appear secondary. But the risks of arbitrary "exclusions" are easy to forsee, especially since they involve the countries of a relatively unstable zone which has experienced profound changes.

By claiming membership to Central Europe, we are not renouncing our traditional ties with the Balkans. We define ourselves as a country in the center of Europe which borders the Balkans, just like Hungary, which also belongs to Central Europe and at the same time borders the countries involved in the Yugoslavian conflict. Part of Romania's specialness lies in its good relations with all the Balkan republics, including those of the former Yugoslavia. This leads us to believe that Romania could play an important role in stabilizing this region, and even in the current efforts to re-establish peace.

That said, it also seems sensible to me, when evaluating Romania's "geostrategic advantage," to take into account its central position between different European regions. We hold an important part of the Black Sea coastline and have the best port facilities. Currently, and especially after the opening of the Rhin-Main-Danube canal, the Danube (which stretches 1000 kilometers with the mouth of the river inside Romania) and the Black Sea can connect Northern and Central Europe with the Caucasus, Central Asian, and Middle Eastern countries.

The change in Romania's geostrategic importance must also be judged in relation to the disappearance of the ideological and political division between East and West. This has allowed Romania to change the direction of its national and foreign policy and to recover its European orientation, to the benefit of the entire continent. Romania's obvious desire to become part of European and Euro-Atlantic structures makes our country an important security factor for use in stabilizing an area whose turbulence could easily place the entire continent in danger. This is a necessary but insufficient condition for integration. In a Europe where interdependence is becoming more important each day, Romania's must resort to inventing customized answers for the politicians and institutions who are counting on the Euro-Atlantic theater, whose choices and decisions must take into account the above ideas.

Last year, the EU, EUO, and NATO gave us more and more encouraging signs, which makes me hope that political leaders have started to discard outdated thought patterns and to understand Romania's geostrategic importance and the role it could play to everyone's benefit.

A buffer zone between two turbulent areas in this part of the world, Romania is today a country on whose stability the entire continent depends. To work towards this stability involves taking into account the lives of hundreds of millions of people who want to live in peace and security. It is in this spirit that I wrote a letter which I sent to all the heads of state of NATO countries at the end of 1993, as well as to the NATO secretary-general, and which is reproduced here in its entirety:

"On the eve of the January 10, 1994 top-level meeting of NATO countries, I would like to restate Romania's position concerning the Atlantic Alliance and its wish to become a full member, as I have already stated in my letter of September 18, 1993 addressed to the Secretary-General of NATO, Mr. Manfred Woerner. Romania considers NATO, whose ability to adapt to post "Cold War" realities has been proven the only organization possible of assuring European stability and guaranteeing the values of democracy and the Constitutional State.

"We welcome with great interest the proposal to associate ourselves with a "Partnership for Peace," which we have evaluated as a preliminary step towards our integration into NATO. My country is willing to participate in this new kind of cooperation and to fully respect the regulations and standards imposed on the members of the Alliance.

"I want to take this opportunity to once again express my belief that as a European State, Romania is entitled to belong to NATO.

"When analyzing our request, please take into consideration Romania's vital security interests which have gained new meaning in the context of the region's recent political developments. In addition, Romania is determined to become more involved in efforts to ensure the region's security and that of Europe in general, and is ready to assume all the responsibilites as a member of NATO.

"I am convinced that Romania's integration into NATO would guarantee Romania the security it needs to accelerate the democratic changes and economic reforms which our society is in the process of carrying out.

"I believe that belonging to NATO is an essential component in Romania's overall process of integration into Euro-Atlantic structures (NATO, EUO, EU, European Council), which constitutes the prime objective of Romania's foreign policy.

"I harbor the hope that in the discussions taking place at the top-level meeting in Brussels, you will consider my country's position, which is supported by the parliamentary political parties as well as by all Romanian people."

As we now know, our request and those of several other countries from this region received the expected response. We signed the first documents concerning the "Partnership for Peace" and we are determined to respect all commitments ensuing from it. In time, our goal is to fulfill the conditions allowing us to become full members of NATO. We are also thinking about the possibility of a "Partnership for Development" and other steps and solutions which would contribute to uniting Central Europe in everyone's best interest, for everyone's greater security and for the development of our economic and political relations.

I would like to add that Romania wishes to end existing conflicts and asks that all necessary actions be taken in order to avert such catastrophes in the future, whose consequences we all suffer. We stress that the United States should remain an important player on the European scene as guarantor of Continental security and stability. For Romania, relations with the United States are still a vital element likely to turn our stability into common capital for the security of the region and the entire continent.

The attempts by people with imperialistic nostalgia to take advantage of the relative confusion generated by the upheavals in Eastern Europe to revive old historical ghosts are explosive and dangerous.

This is why we consider it in the national interest of each of the region's countries to contribute to the stability and democratic development of all the others; in short, it is not difficult to understand that in a stormy ocean no one can find refuge on an island.

We should not assume from this that Romania is not interested in developing similar relations with countries from other continents which may not be our immediate neighbors. In a world where modern communication techniques have spectacularly shrunk distances, these countries with whom we share the same concerns about the development of contemporary society and the future of civilization are still our neighbors. Nevertheless, Romanian foreign policy strategies are determined by the immediate environment and this demands answers to serious and objective questions which we cannot ignore without placing all of Europe, and possibly the entire world, in danger.

Conclusion:
The Politician and the Challenges
of the Contemporary World

As a politician, I find myself confronted with two challenges, a situation which is not easy to manage on the conceptional level. I strive to not let my mind get muddled up by imprecise and inconcrete ideas and to give clear answers to practical questions. Being open-minded allows me to constantly question my own opinions, without losing myself in useless speculations, and to have simple and direct relationships with people.

The collapse of the Soviet System was an unprecedented moment in history, a monumental change of a magnitude never seen before. On the road leading from State communism to democracy and a market economy, there is no model, no guide and almost no landmarks.

The totalitarian system which covered such a large part of the planet, fed by ideological fantasies and an abuse of trust, has recently caved in. Most of the ruins, still warm under the smoking ashes, are found here, in this part of the world.

The first challenge is not so much the revolution itself, but the ability to succeed in getting rid of the garbage we have inherited and imagining a new horizon; it's a totally new experience in which the actors are looking for cues. We are in the middle of crossing an unknown ocean, perhaps to discover a new world. We are all in a period of transition and must invent a new political structure to find our way out. Of course our countries were freed from totalitarianism, but so was the rest of the world. We have started on our way, we are already on the road, but where are we headed? Can we have faith in the unknown? History never repeats itself and we can at least be sure to have put an end once and for all to the totalitarian social and political system. But to be sure of which shore we are headed for and when we will get there is another question, an existential question to which we have no precise answers, because these answers will come from the work of several generations.

And the politician?

He finds himself confronted with another challenge which this time concerns him directly. He must change his perception of the world, his attitude toward what is real and he must revise how he operates within the new social and political structures. I believe that we are the first generation of politicians to have to run a global political system which is no longer a simple structure, but a cybernetic model with multiple variants. This task is infinitely more complex. This system must be continually adapted in order to run smoothly as no one person has sole control over it; each party must preserve its own dynamic and at the same time join in the general project.

Since the beginning of time, the world policy of several large and powerful States consisted in simply wanting to include others within the borders of their power in order to impose a supposedly better system on them, as it was more efficient in terms of strength. As for the small countries, it was about resistance. Even the policies of the superpowers' and the "blocks" envisioned the eventual destruction of one another, forced to adopt the adversary's social and political system. It was the condition of supposed global harmony, obtained through the reduction of opposites.

In this second half of the 20th century, the evolution of techniques is transforming the planet into a global village and making us rub shoulders with numerous very different civilizations and systems; thus, total standardization seems inconceivable. We have lost confidence in universal models and it is only today that our mindset has sufficiently evolved to teach us to celebrate others' differences, to understand and respect individuals, communities, countries and peoples and what makes them special, what makes them different from us, without attempting to force them to ressemble us.

Up until now, politicians have never suggested considering the evolution of a world where a series of independent structures following their own logical development must be directed as a whole. Though it is imperative to recognize the fundamental differences between the political and social systems, we absolutely must find a balance, if only to save the earth from catastrophes – not necessarily military disasters, but equally dangerous ecological and economic ones which could have unknown social and political consequences. How can we not worry when we hear that last year, according to international authorities, 100 million men and women left their homelands to look for an new country likely to accept, house and feed them? How can we ignore that a single fair administration of the worlds' problems would prevent a tidalwave capable of throwing us back into the barbarity of the stampede and putting all of contemporary civilization in danger? How can we not worry when we observe that in a world full of turmoil, where unexpected and uncontrollabe changes happen so quickly, what we gain on one side we can lose on the other? As soon as the Iron Curtain disappeared, it was replaced by another just as dangerous and unbearable economic one.

We are confronted with specific challenges in this part of the world. This has always been the case. Romania has always been in "transition," with highs and lows lasting several centuries or just a generation or two but always in the middle of a continual and difficult process of dramatic change. Throughout our history, we have never had the chance to see natural cycles of development as we were forced to function according to foreign pressure. Today we finally have the chance to live a totally different historic reality. We can build a society without bowing to foreign pressures and with hope of having a rest period to allow development to take place in accordance with our society's natural demands.

The balances which we have to preserve within Romanian society are also those of all humanity, our basic structures overlapping to give birth to a new global social order. This birth is so engrained in nature that it cannot be hindered but runs the risk of taking place in the peril of catastrophy if we cannot offer it the conditions of a controlled and easy evolution.

History is created in the laboratories of political structures and it challenges us to succeed in doing in Romania today that which the world will be forced to do in the near future. We must first create a balance between the shattered social components (a state which allows them to be shown with a bareness we often forget) which sometimes violently conflict with another. And we must create this balance, maintaining the smooth functioning of the capitalist dynamic in mind and, at the same time, preserving social peace. We must also preserve general peace at a time when the resurgence of nationalism is making Romania a buffer zone between two zones of conflict. We also have to maintain the security of Romania, a recent ex-"block" country, in this world full of accumulated tensions which create a climate of fear where people wait for political leaders to propose original solutions to their problems.

For the Romanians, the Revolution was a sort of absolution, a chance to recover their diginity and show themselves as they really are and how they have gone through History, fed by a profound desire for freedom and identity. Romanians are a people who, time after time, proved their inclination toward peace, their sense of balance and their respect for others. However weighty our heritage is, however deep the wounds the Revolution left which we continue to pay for, aware of the effort that lies ahead, we have good reason to look toward the future with confidence. With all that is most profound in my soul, with all of the strength of conviction that I am capable of, I believe that Romania is in the process of rebirth and will soon find its true image of light and peace.

Demographic Data on Romania, According to National, Social, Religious and Growth Trends: Based on Statistics from 1977 to 1992

The population's structure in millions of inhabitants
divided by social group (urban and rural), based on census information
from 1930, 1948, 1956, 1966, 1977, 1992

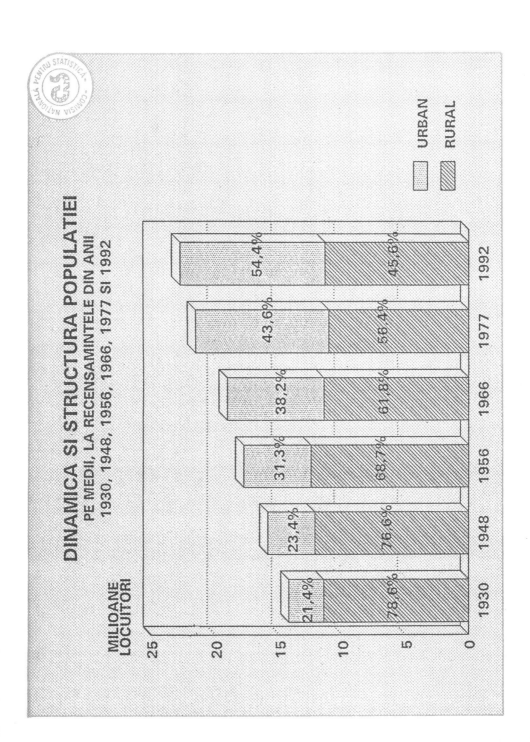

DINAMICA SI STRUCTURA POPULATIEI
PE MEDII, LA RECENSAMINTELE DIN ANII
1930, 1948, 1956, 1966, 1977 SI 1992

MILIOANE
LOCUITORI

URBAN
RURAL

1930   1948   1956   1966   1977   1992

21,4%   23,4%   31,3%   38,2%   43,6%   54,4%
78,6%   76,6%   68,7%   61,8%   56,4%   45,6%

Population by department, according to the 1992 census
compared with the 1977 census
(increase or decrease compared to 1977 in %)

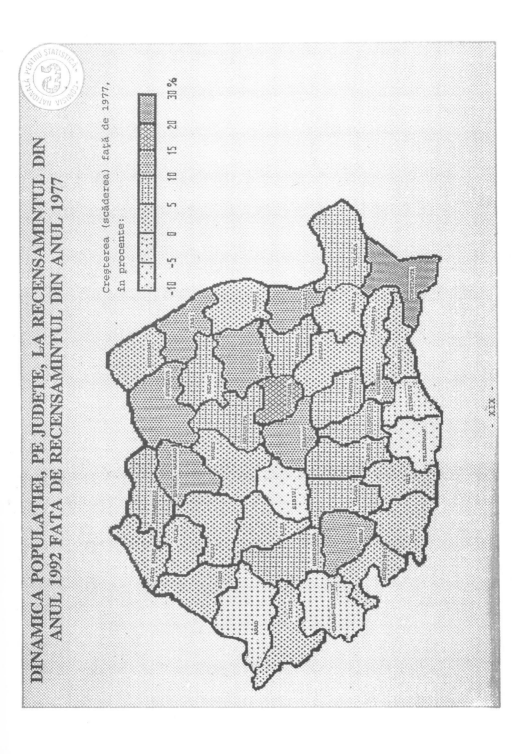

DINAMICA POPULAȚIEI, PE JUDEȚE, LA RECENSAMÎNTUL DIN
ANUL 1992 FAȚA DE RECENSAMÎNTUL DIN ANUL 1977

Creșterea (scăderea) fața de 1977,
în procente:

-10 -5 0 5 10 15 20 30 %

- XIX -

The population density based on the 1992 census

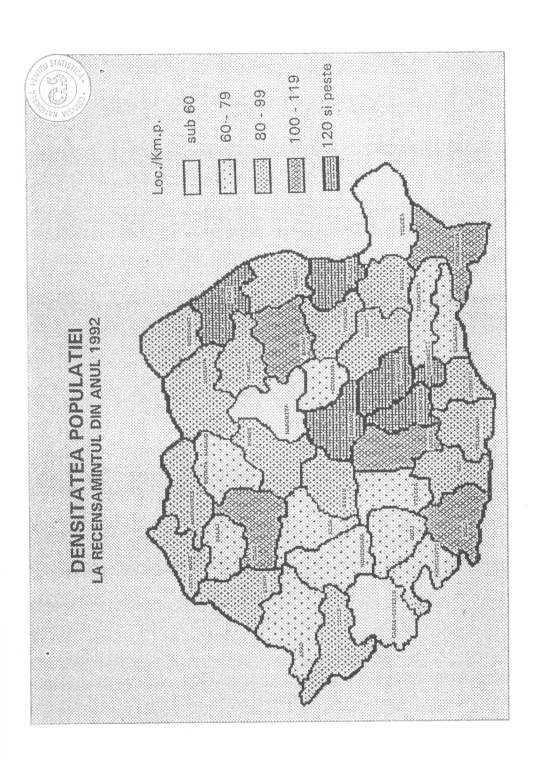

DENSITATEA POPULATIEI
LA RECENSAMINTUL DIN ANUL 1992

Loc./Km.p.

sub 60
60 - 79
80 - 99
100 - 119
120 si peste

Percentage of the urban population based on the 1977 and 1992 census, by department

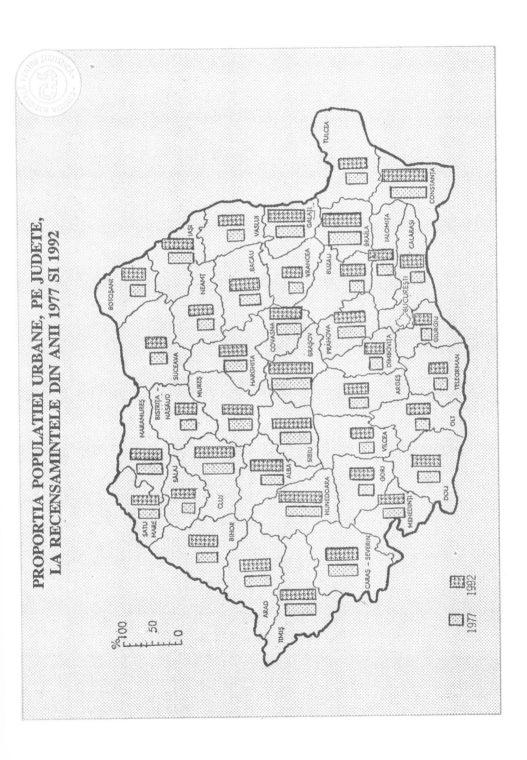

PROPORTIA POPULATIEI URBANE, PE JUDETE,
LA RECENSAMINTELE DIN ANII 1977 SI 1992

The distribution of the population according to the principal ethnicities (Romanians, Hungarians, Gypsies, Germans and others)

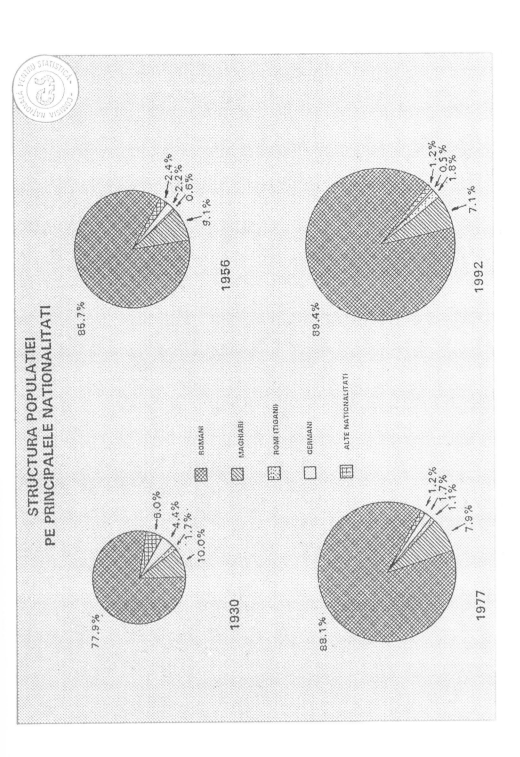

STRUCTURA POPULATIEI
PE PRINCIPALELE NATIONALITATI

ROMANI

MAGHIARI

ROMI (TIGANI)

GERMANI

ALTE NATIONALITATI

1956

86.7%

2.4%
2.2%
0.6%
9.1%

1992

89.4%

1.2%
0.5%
1.8%
7.1%

1930

77.9%

6.0%
4.4%
1.7%
10.0%

1977

88.1%

1.2%
1.7%
1.1%
7.9%

The population make-up in millions according to the principal ethnicities, based on the 1992 census, by department (in % of Romanians, Hungarians, and other ethnicities)

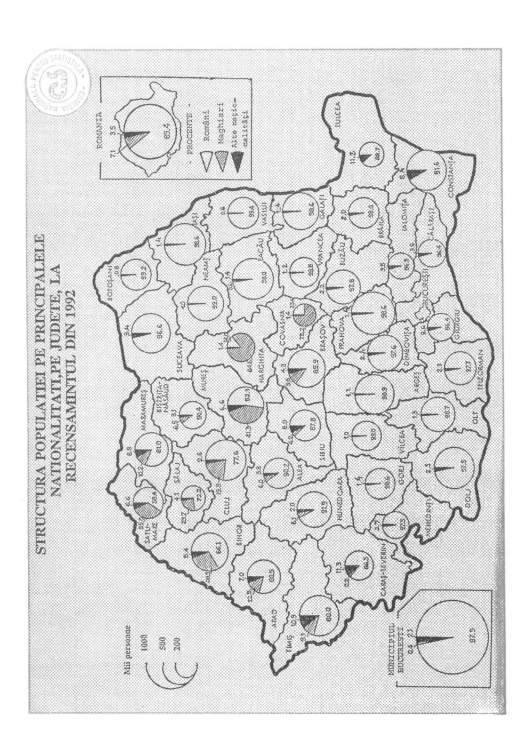

STRUCTURA POPULAȚIEI PE PRINCIPALELE NAȚIONALITĂȚI,PE JUDEȚE, LA RECENSĂMÎNTUL DIN 1992

The distribution of the population according to the principal religions practiced, based on the 1930 and 1992 censuses

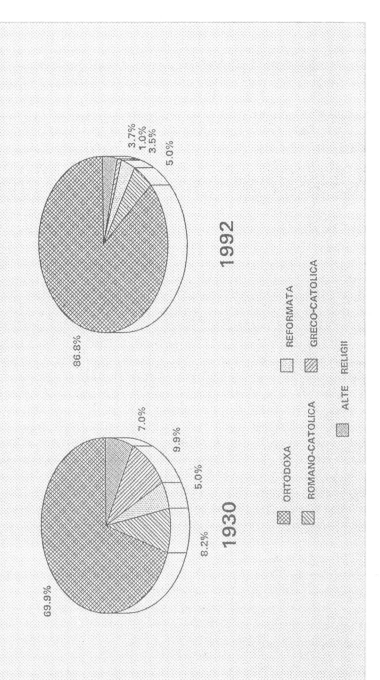

STRUCTURA POPULATIEI PE PRINCIPALELE
RELIGII LA RECENSAMINTELE DIN ANII
1930 SI 1992

1930

1992

69.9%
8.2%
5.0%
9.9%
7.0%

86.8%
3.7%
1.0%
3.5%
5.0%

ORTODOXA

ROMANO-CATOLICA

ALTE RELIGII

REFORMATA

GRECO-CATOLICA

The average family size, based on the 1992 census, by department

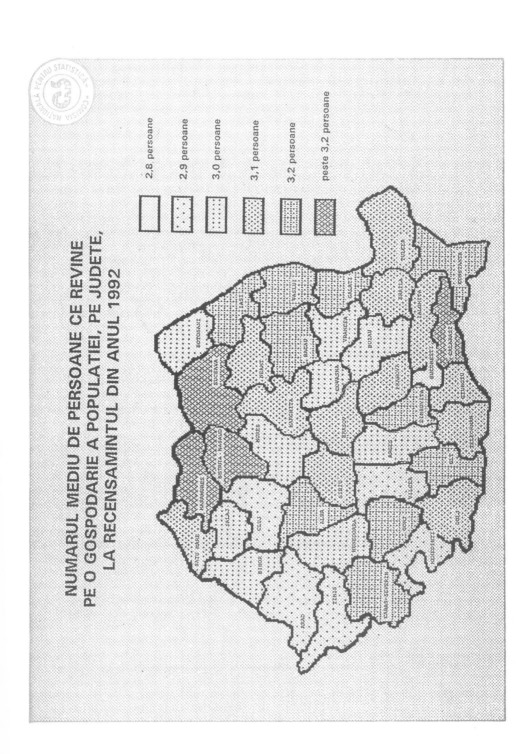

NUMARUL MEDIU DE PERSOANE CE REVINE
PE O GOSPODARIE A POPULATIEI, PE JUDETE,
LA RECENSAMINTUL DIN ANUL 1992

2,8 persoane

2,9 persoane

3,0 persoane

3,1 persoane

3,2 persoane

peste 3,2 persoane

Housing comparison (rural-urban) between the 1977 and 1992 censuses
(houses, lodging rooms and inhabitable space)

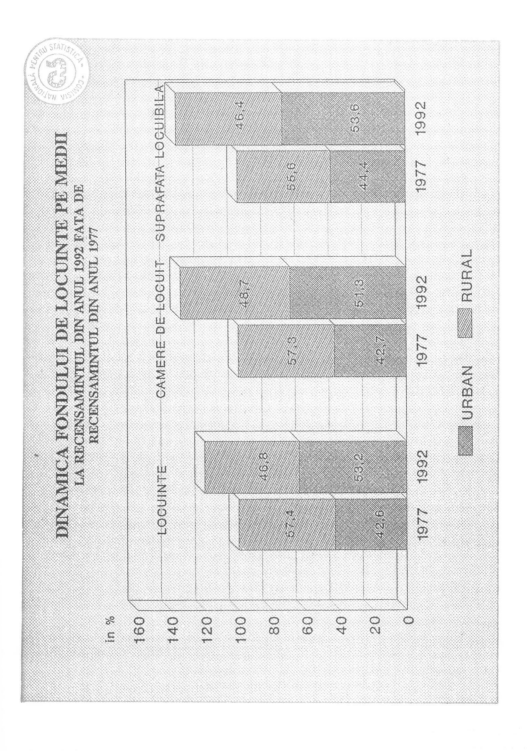

DINAMICA FONDULUI DE LOCUINTE PE MEDII
LA RECENSAMINTUL DIN ANUL 1992 FATA DE
RECENSAMINTUL DIN ANUL 1977

Housing comparison based on heating methods, according to the 1977 and 1992 census (thermal power station and central heating, gas, and other methods)

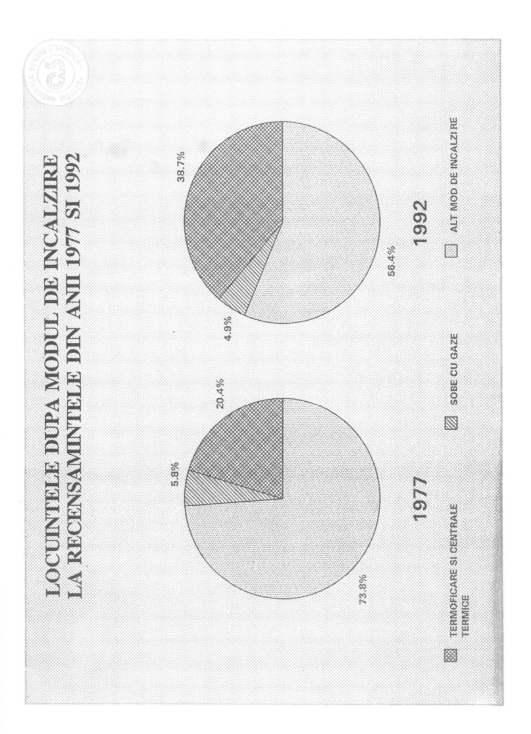

LOCUINTELE DUPA MODUL DE INCALZIRE
LA RECENSAMINTELE DIN ANII 1977 SI 1992

1977

73.8%

5.8%

20.4%

1992

56.4%

4.9%

38.7%

TERMOFICARE SI CENTRALE TERMICE

SOBE CU GAZE

ALT MOD DE INCALZIRE

Chronological Summary
of Romanian History

70-44 B.C. - The sovereign Chief Burebista unites the Getaean and Dacian tribes, laying the foundations for the centralized Dac State.

87-106 - Under the reign of King Decebal, the authority of the Dac State stretches from what is now Transylvania, Banat and Oltenia to the eastern oriental Carpathian Mountains. 101-103 and 105-106 are marked by Daco-Roman invasion wars, following which the Romans occupy Sarmisegetusa, the country's capital, and the King commits suicide.

106-271 - The Roman occupation in the country of Dac gives rise, through the crossing of the two populations, to the Romanian people.

850-1200 - Appearance and consolidation of the first Romanian sovereriegn states in the provinces today called Transylvania, Banat, Maramures, Crisana, Oltenia, Dobruja and Moldova.

1310-1359 - Birth of the Romanian feudal States of Muntenia and Moldova under the Basarabe and Musatin dynasties.

1599-1601 - King Mihai the Great succeeds in uniting Muntenia, Translyvania and Moldova.

1775 - Northern Moldova, Bukovina is annexed by the Hapsburg Empire.

1784 - Large peasant, social and national uprising by Transylvanian Romanians, a movement led by Horea, Closca and Crisan.

1812 - The south-eastern part of Moldova is annexed by the Czarist Empire.

1821 - The revolutionary movement led by Tudor Vladimirescu in Muntenia marks the begining of the modern period.

1848-1849 - Political, social and national revolutions in Muntenia, Moldova and Transylvania.

1859-1866 - Under the reign of Alexander Ioan Cuza, birth of the national modern State through the unification on January 24, 1859 of the pricipalities of Moldova and Muntenia.

1867 - Transylvania is annexed by the Austro-Hungarian Empire.

1866-1914 - Creation of the first Romanian Constitution under the reign of Carol de Hohenzollern in 1866.

1877 -Achieved total independence.

1878 -Dobruja united with Romania and the re-annexation of southern Bessarabia by the Russian Empire (which since the Paris treaty of 1858 became part of Moldova).

1918 - Following World War I, reunification of Bessarabia on March 27, of Bukovina on November 28, of Transylvania, Banat, Crisana, and the Maramures on December 1st.

1919-1920 - Through the peace treaties signed at Saint-Germaine in 1919 and at Trianon and Paris in 1920, Romania's reunification gains international recognition.

1938-1940 - King Carol II establishes a dictatorship, then abdicates in favor of his son who legitimizes a national legionnaire State.

1940 - Following the Ribbentrop-Molotov German-Soviet non-aggression pact, Romania's forced dismemberment begins. On June 27, after the "Molotov Ultimatum" Romania sees itself forced to give up Bessarabia and northern Bukovina to the Soviet Union. On August

30, the second "Vienna Arbitration" dictates the removal of northern Transylvania from Romania. On September 7, in accordance with Bulgaro-Romanian treaty at Craiova, southern Dobruja becomes part of Bulgaria.

1941 - General Ion Antonescu establishes a military dictatorship and has Romania participate in World War II on the side of the Axis powers to reunify Romania. Bessarabia and northern Bukovina rejoin Romania (but will again become part of the Soviet Union).

1944 - August 23, the Romanian army joins the Allied forces. The Eastern and Western military campaigns will cost Romania more than half a million dead and a considerable economic effort. On September 12, signing in Moscow of the armistice agreement between the Romanian government and the Allied governments, through which the "treaty of Vienna" is repealed, among others.

1945 - March 6, government established led by Petru Groza, dominated by the communists.

1945 - October, Gheorghe Gheorghiu-Dej is elected secretary-general of the Romanian Communist Party Central Committee.

1947 - February 10, the Romanian government signes the peace treaty in Paris with the Allied powers.

1947 - July-December, the "traditional" parties are dissolved. King Michael is forced to abdicate and the monarchy is abolished. Proclamation of the Romanian Popular Republic.

1953-1957 - Gheorghe Gheorghiu-Dej, the communist leader, serves as President of the Council of Ministers.

1961 - March, the "Presidium of the Great National Assembly" is replaced by the Council of the State, whose president is Gheorghe Gheorghiu-Dej, with the Prime Minister being Ion Gheorghe Maurer.

1964 - April 15-22, the Romanian Communist Party Central Committee adopts "the declaration concerning the Romanian Communist Party's position within the scope of international workers' communist movements," thus distancing itself from the USSR's hegemony.

1965 - March 22, Nicolae Ceaucescu is elected First Secretary of Romanian Communist Party Central Committee following the death of Gheoghe Gheorghiu-Dej on March 19.

1968 - August, Romania publicly condemns the invasion of Czechoslovakia by Warsaw Pact forces.

1971-1974 - After a period of relative freedom, especially economic freedom, Romania enters into a period of stagnation and great difficulties.

1974 - Nicolae Ceaucescu also takes hold of the country's presidency, called from now on a Socialist Republic. It is the beginning of his dictatorship.

1989 - December 22, the Romanian Revolution is unleashed, which ends Nicolae Ceacescu's communist dictatorship.

On the evening of December 22, 1989, radio and television broadcast "The Call to the Nation," the first document drawn up by the Council of the National Salvation Front, new organization which henceforth assumed power, with Ion Iliescu elected to lead it.

1990 - February 1, creation of the Provisional Council for National Unity, with representatives from all the parties created since 1989, as well as representatives for ethnic minorities. The president of this new organization is Ion Iliescu.

1990 - May 20, the first free presidential as well as parliamentary elections took place. The bicameral parliament and the Chamber of Deputies and the Senate draw up and adopt a new Romanian constitution. With 85% of the vote, Ion Iliescu is elected president of Romania.

1991 - August 28, after the disintegration of the Soviet Union, the Republic of Moldova proclaims its independence.

1991 - December 8, a national referendum on the new constitution approved by the Parliament is submitted to the voters.

1992 - February, elections for the municipal councils with the participation of all the parties formed after the Revolution.

1992 - September-October, parliamentary and presidential elections with the participation of numerous parties, some of them banding together to form the "Democratic Convention." For the second time, Ion Iliescu is elected president of Romania.

Table of contents